Cambridge Ele

Elements in Public Policy
edited by
M. Ramesh
National University of Singapore (NUS)
Michael Howlett
Simon Fraser University, British Columbia
Xun WU
Hong Kong University of Science and Technology (Guangzhou)
Judith Clifton
University of Cantabria
Eduardo Araral
National University of Singapore (NUS)

PUBLIC CONTRACTING FOR SOCIAL OUTCOMES

Clare J FitzGerald
King's College London
J Ruairi Macdonald
University of Oxford

Shaftesbury Road, Cambridge CB2 8EA, United Kingdom

One Liberty Plaza, 20th Floor, New York, NY 10006, USA

477 Williamstown Road, Port Melbourne, VIC 3207, Australia

314–321, 3rd Floor, Plot 3, Splendor Forum, Jasola District Centre, New Delhi – 110025, India

103 Penang Road, #05–06/07, Visioncrest Commercial, Singapore 238467

Cambridge University Press is part of Cambridge University Press & Assessment, a department of the University of Cambridge.

We share the University's mission to contribute to society through the pursuit of education, learning and research at the highest international levels of excellence.

www.cambridge.org
Information on this title: www.cambridge.org/9781009486828

DOI: 10.1017/9781108953887

© Clare J FitzGerald and J Ruairi Macdonald 2024

This publication is in copyright. Subject to statutory exception and to the provisions of relevant collective licensing agreements, with the exception of the Creative Commons version the link for which is provided below, no reproduction of any part may take place without the written permission of Cambridge University Press & Assessment.

An online version of this work is published at doi.org/10.1017/9781108953887 under a Creative Commons Open Access license CC-BY-NC-ND 4.0 which permits re-use, distribution and reproduction in any medium for non-commercial purposes providing appropriate credit to the original work is given. You may not distribute derivative works without permission. To view a copy of this license, visit https://creativecommons.org/licenses/by-nc-nd/4.0

When citing this work, please include a reference to the DOI 10.1017/9781108953887

First published 2024

A catalogue record for this publication is available from the British Library.

ISBN 978-1-009-48682-8 Hardback
ISBN 978-1-108-94897-5 Paperback
ISSN 2398-4058 (online)
ISSN 2514-3565 (print)

Cambridge University Press & Assessment has no responsibility for the persistence or accuracy of URLs for external or third-party internet websites referred to in this publication and does not guarantee that any content on such websites is, or will remain, accurate or appropriate.

Public Contracting for Social Outcomes

Elements in Public Policy

DOI: 10.1017/9781108953887
First published online: December 2024

Clare J FitzGerald
King's College London

J Ruairi Macdonald
University of Oxford

Author for correspondence: Clare J FitzGerald, clare.fitzgerald@kcl.ac.uk

Abstract: Governments all over the world have transitioned away from directly providing public services to contracting and collaborating with cross-sectoral networks to deliver services on their behalf. Governments have thus pursued an array of policy instruments to improve interorganizational progress towards policy goals. In recent years, outcomes-based contracting has emerged as a compelling solution to service quality shortcomings and collective action challenges. Informed by public policy, public administration, and public procurement scholarship, this Element details the evolution of social outcomes in public contracting, exploring the relationship between how outcomes are specified and managed and how well such instruments deliver against policy goals. It comments on the possible drawbacks of contracting for social outcomes, highlighting how governments may use outcomes as an excuse to avoid actively managing contracts or to sidestep their accountability as outlined in public law. This title is also available as Open Access on Cambridge Core.

Keywords: policy implementation, public contracting, public procurement, policy design, outcomes-based contracting

© Clare J FitzGerald and J Ruairi Macdonald 2024

ISBNs: 9781009486828 (HB), 9781108948975 (PB), 9781108953887 (OC)
ISSNs: 2398-4058 (online), 2514-3565 (print)

Contents

1 Introduction   1

2 The Evolution of Public Contracting   4

3 Public Procurement   20

4 Outcomes-Based Contracting   32

5 Conclusion   53

   References   61

1 Introduction

Public contracting accounts for almost a third of government expenditure within the OECD, amounting to about 13 per cent of GDP on average (OECD, 2021). Contracts underpin the delivery of health, education, and general public services, which combined account for over two-thirds of public procurement spending (OECD, 2021). Globally, the value of public contracts is estimated at over $13 trillion annually, exclusive of public procurement during the Covid-19 crisis (Hunt, 2020; Makgill, Yeung and Marchessault, 2020).

In countries the world over, governments have transitioned away from directly providing public services to contracting and collaborating with third parties to deliver services on their behalf. Dense, multilevel, and cross-sectoral governance networks typify public service provision in places like the US and the UK (Koliba et al., 2019), a reality that scholars have variously referred to as the 'hollow' state, the 'contracting' state, the 'enabling' state, and a 'state of agents' (Hood, 1995; Kirkpatrick and Lucio, 1996; Milward, 1996; Milward and Provan, 2000; Heinrich, Lynn and Milward, 2010; Sainsbury, 2013). Sometimes, these arrangements are highly formalised – as in public–private partnerships. Other times, they are amalgamations of bilateral agreements with little planned interconnectivity.

While public contracts have long played a major role in industrial development, including innovations in flight and the internet (Nagle, 1999, 2012), the ascent of privatisation and shift away from direct bureaucratic provision starting in the 1980s has been hotly debated amongst academics, public managers, the public, and politicians alike. Involving private and nonprofit actors in the business of government means delegating discretion and authority away from the state, forcing ideological and normative argumentation about which activities are inherently governmental and which can be reasonably delivered via the market.

Economists often argue that government involvement is meant to correct for market failures like externalities and collective goods (Lazzarini, 2022). Using regulations, rewards, and sanctions, governments can curtail bad behaviours – like pollution – and promote good ones – like fair labour practices. Likewise, through taxation, governments can produce an adequate supply of collective goods like national parks or national defence, which if left to market provision would be in short supply due to low-paid demand (Lazzarini, 2022).

Governments, however, are not without their limitations. In delivering collective goods deemed worthwhile by a majority, governments can struggle to provide support to the minority. The somewhat adversarial nature of electoral democracy likewise means that members of the public face significant hurdles when challenging poor public performance. Government-monopolised public service provision lacks competitive pressure and direct performance indicators, creating concern that states are structurally disposed to expand provision and inflate costs, running counter to public interest as defined by measures of efficiency (Wolf, 1979; Grand, 1991; Weber, 2014).

Given the options – the inefficiencies of government or the inequalities of the market – practitioners and academics alike have sought an ideal counterpoise: harnessing the ruthless efficiency of the private sector while enhancing public value considerations of quality, equity, reviewability, and accountability. As the preferred tool of privatisation, the design of public contracts has been a critical mechanism through which states have tried to achieve such a balance (Van Slyke, 2003).

As predicted by Le Grand, the result of government-subsidised intervention through contracts has been mixed (1991). While early rhetoric regarding contracting out was alarmist (Salamon, 1989), later research focused more so on conceptual clarification and executing 'empirical tests of the implications of changing governance configurations against various criteria, including equity in access to public goods and services, responsiveness to "customers" (formerly "clients" or "patients"), accountability to elected officials and organized stakeholders, efficiency in service provision, and effectiveness in producing outcomes and results' (Heinrich, Lynn and Milward, 2010, p. i4).

A 2018 systematic review of the economic and quality effects of contracting out showed that the cost savings associated with outsourcing have decreased over time, are greater for technical services (e.g., waste collection, building maintenance, water services, public transit) than for social services (e.g., mental health, nursing homes, employment support, children's residential care), and have been twice as large in 'Anglo-Saxon' countries as compared to those with higher bargaining coverage. The review also highlighted a concerning lack of information on the effects of contracting out on service quality and limited use of measures of transaction costs, making it difficult to assess the influence of outsourcing on the overall cost-effectiveness of service delivery (Petersen, Hjelmar and Vrangbæk, 2018). Combined, the findings suggest that 'generalization of effects from contracting out should be made with caution and are likely to depend, among other things, on the transaction cost characteristics of the service, the market situation, and the institutional/regulatory setting' (Petersen, Hjelmar and Vrangbæk, 2018, p. 130). Other research shows that the decision to contract out can be influenced by ideology, suggesting that social services more so than technical ones 'are the contemporary ideological battlefield of privatization' (Petersen, Houlberg and Christensen, 2015, p. 560).

This Element is an exploration of public contracting mostly in health and social services, representing an authoritative, but not exhaustive, review of relevant public administration, public procurement, and public policy literature from the UK and the US. In it, we situate public contracting as a meso- and micro-level element of macro-level public governance paradigms, building theory and advancing a cross-disciplinary understanding about how the specification of contracts through procurement strengthens or weakens links between policy design and implementation (Howlett, Ramesh and Capano, 2022, 2023). We also underscore the oft overlooked role of public procurement as a strategic function of government, charged with designing and managing contracts in pursuit of wider policy objectives while upholding fundamental values rooted in public law: transparency, accountability, equal treatment, due process, and fair competition.

It is our contention that public procurement operationalises policy goals and objectives through the delegation of authority, the specification of incentives and monitoring, and the articulation of governance mechanisms within contracts, enabling organisations from across sectors to advance the public interest. To illustrate the argument, we explore opportunities, complexities, and tensions in outcomes-based contracting (OBC), a novel approach to public service contracting which ties payment to the achievement of social outcomes and advances 'increased and sometimes novel inter-sectoral relationships between governments, nonprofits, and for-profit organisations' (FitzGerald et al., 2023a, p. 329).

In Section 2, we trace the macro-level evolution of public contracting across public governance paradigms. We describe the history and process of privatisation via contracting, from the bureaucracies of Traditional Public Administration to the reforms of New Public Management and the advent of New Public Governance. We reflect the collaborative turn in contemporary public management which emphasises relational over technical mechanisms to govern the cross-sectoral networks that interdependently deliver health and social services today. The section then tracks changes in approaches to public contracting over time, charting shifts in the specification of incentives and monitoring from efficiency-seeking bipartite fee-for-service contracts to contemporary multilateral outcomes-based contracts ambitiously designed to facilitate collective action and improve public service performance.

In Section 3, we turn to the role of public procurement professionals and their influence on the design, award, and management of public contracts. This section describes procurement professionals as specialised public managers operating in rules-based environments. We distil three layers of rules within which procurement professionals operate: overarching principles; links to wider economic, social, and environmental policies; and rules directly related to contract performance. The section details the growing discretion and responsibility given to procurement professionals to design and manage public contracts that are explicitly linked to wider policy objectives – for example sustainability targets, social equity considerations, and specified social outcomes. We further note that public contracts have traditionally hinged upon management of inputs, activities, and outputs presumed to lead to outcomes and that tensions can arise in OBC when the role of government is limited to approving a fixed payment for their achievement.

Section 4 addresses OBC more directly and details the ways in which outcomes are specified in contracts. In addition to reviewing the evidence on OBC, we frame outcomes-based contracts as tools which determine micro-dimensions of policies – their specifications or 'on the ground requirements' and calibrations or 'ways of delivery' (Howlett, Ramesh and Capano, 2023). Detailing contractual specifications in light of the policy goals which illuminate them thickens contemporary decompositional approaches to policy studies and forces scholars to consider not just whether a service should be contracted out but also *how* it has been contracted out. We explore these nuances in the design of two Outcomes Funds, an increasingly popular policy approach to supporting multiple and simultaneous outcomes-based contracts. Using the UK Department for Work in Pensions Innovation Fund and the Department for Digital, Culture, Media and Sport Life Chances Fund, we compare and contrast how the UK central government has specified and calibrated Outcomes Funds in relation to payable outcomes, outcomes validation methods, and the discretion given to other parties in the contract. Using published qualitative and quantitative evaluation material, we then compare their performance against articulated policy goals and objectives.

Finally, in Section 5, we discuss the broader implications for public accountability when the focus of oversight is on outcomes rather than processes. We provide practical commentary on the necessity of having adequate capacity within government to oversee outcomes-based contracts if they are to improve public service delivery and advance of policy objectives. We also underscore important ramifications around a loss of democratic anchorage and the potential for outcomes to enable governments to abscond from their public duties. In closing, we highlight the critical importance of recognising inherently governmental functions even when contracting for social outcomes.

2 The Evolution of Public Contracting

In the pre-war period, states were largely organised into bureaucracies. In an ideal bureaucracy, governments were organised around hierarchical line management of subordinates by supervisors, relationships encapsulated in fixed jurisdictions ordered by rules, laws, or regulations. It was the holding of office, not the individuals themselves, from which the authority to issue commands was tied. Office holders were selected based on expertise and training, rather than patronage, and enjoyed stable, long-term, full-time, decently salaried positions with good pensions. A hallmark of bureaucratic management was record-keeping as a mechanism for ensuring equitable decisions – especially social service access – and preserving organisational memory. Thus, holding public office was characterised as a vocation with its own training, duties, and values (Weber, Gerth and Mills, 1948; Pollitt, 2009; Torfing et al., 2020). Structured this way, under a governance paradigm now referred to as Traditional Public Administration (TPA), bureaucracies were seen to function as safeguards against tyranny and protectors of due process according to the constitution. Their advancement throughout the nineteenth and twentieth centuries was largely based on their 'technical superiority over any other form of organization', especially in organising and delivering high-volume standardised tasks (Weber, Gerth and Mills, 1948).

In practice, however, bureaucracies had their drawbacks. They were thought to encourage instrumental rationality at the expense of substantive rationality, encouraging rule following over results and emphasising accountability for processes rather than results. This emphasis on process meant that bureaucracies had a penchant for creating more rules to make existing rules less ambiguous, stripping innovation and energy from daily work and removing incentives to encourage higher performance resulting in a lifeless 'iron cage' (Weber, Gerth and Mills, 1948). If left unchecked, bureaucracies were thought to grow indefinitely regardless of whether actual workload increased, and they were seen to be poor at coping with uncertain environments, new tasks, and horizontal ways of working: their competence within jurisdictional silos offset by an inability to speak across departments or agencies.

2.1 Privatisation

By the end of the 1970s, the old social democratic order was in crisis and bureaucratic challenge was on the rise. With economic stagflation and widespread strikes by large public sector trade unions, the growing middle classes of the US and UK began to resent high taxation and became disenchanted with large post-war welfare states. Concerns about politicians favouring expansionist public agencies advanced the introduction of public choice theory where government failure was characterised as endless public bloat necessitating continually growing tax levels but poor economic performance (Boston, 2011; Ferlie, 2017; Niskanen, 2017). In the words of the Trilateral Commission, the 'large public sectors in the Western world were "overloaded" with problems and demands' and 'society and the economy were becoming more "ungovernable"' (Torfing et al., 2020 quoting Crozier et al., 1975).

The solution to the problem of government was to shift the production of welfare to the private sector, 'increasing the reliance on self-regulating markets and communities' (Torfing et al., 2020, p. 55). This milieux, combined with small-state political rhetoric, gave birth to a suite of reforms meant to shrink the size of direct government action and introduce the discipline of private markets and management, a public governance paradigm called New Public Management (NPM) (Torfing et al., 2020). NPM reforms are strongly associated with the political rise of the New Right and were famously pursued by UK Prime Minister Margaret Thatcher, who served from 1979 to 1990, and two-term US President Ronald Reagan, first elected in 1980 (Ferlie, 2017).

NPM functioned on the logic that government bureaucracies routinely failed to achieve economic and organisational efficiency (Hefetz and Warner, 2004). Though loosely coupled, NPM reforms promulgated the notion that government failure could be mitigated by shades of market involvement. Large welfare programmes were scaled down, marginal tax rates were slashed, and 'privatization and contracting out' were pursued alongside 'marketization of services still inside the public sector' and the strengthening of 'performance management and managerialization' (Boston, 2011; Ferlie, 2017, p. 2). In his paper 'A Public Management for all Seasons?' Christopher Hood provided a list of seven doctrinal components of NPM, condensing the core logics of the bureaucratic reforms which have dominated OECD countries since the late 1980s (see Table 1) (Aucoin, 1990; Pollitt, 1990; Hood, 1991). Ewan Ferlie likewise distilled NPM into three 'M's: i) *markets* and quasi-markets; ii) *management* within agencies; and iii) *measurement* of performance (Ferlie, 2017).

Market reforms included the privatisation of nationalised industries like public utilities, the outsourcing of public services to third parties, and the creation of 'quasi-markets' for those services still directly delivered by government. For example, the introduction of the internal market to the National Health Service in 1991 separated purchasers (i.e., health authorities and general practice fundholders) from providers (i.e., hospitals and community health service providers) and charged the former with 'seeking the most cost-effective forms of care for their local population' by 'contracting with hospitals and community health Trusts to provide necessary care' (Rosen and Mays, 1998, p. 105) – indicative of doctrines four and five (Ferlie et al., 1996; Ferlie, 2017).

Management reforms focused on disaggregating and downsizing bureaucracies (e.g., Next Steps Initiative), exporting operations into executive agencies that were then performance managed from above by political principals (Ferlie, 2017, p. 2). This marked a purposeful step-change from the security of rule- and

Table 1 Doctrinal components of New Public Management

NPM Doctrine	Meaning	Typical Justification
1. Hands on professional management in the public sector	Active, visible, discretionary control of organisations from named persons at the top, 'free to manage'	Accountability requires clear assignment of responsibility for action, not diffusion of power
2. Explicit standards and measures of performance	Definition of goals, targets, indicators of success, preferably expressed in quantitative terms, especially for professional services	Accountability requires clear statement of goals; efficiency requires 'hard look' at objectives
3. Greater emphasis on output controls	Resource allocation and rewards linked to measured performance; breakup of centralised bureaucracy-wide personnel management	Need to stress *results* rather than *procedures*
4. Shift to disaggregation of units in the public sector	Break up of formerly 'monolithic' units, unbundling of unitary form management systems into corporatised units around products, operating on decentralised 'one-line' budgets and dealing with one another on an 'arms-length' basis	Need to create 'manageable' units, separate *provision* and *production* interests, gain efficiency advantages of use of contract or franchise arrangements *inside* as well as outside the public sector

Table 1 (cont.)

NPM Doctrine	Meaning	Typical Justification
5. Shift to greater competition in the public sector	Move to term contracts and public tendering procedures	*Rivalry* as the key to lower costs and better standards
6. Stress on private sector styles of management practice	Move away from military-style 'public service ethic', greater flexibility in hiring and rewards, greater use of PR techniques	Need to use 'proven' private sector management tools in the public service
7. Stress on greater discipline and parsimony in resource use	Cutting direct costs, raising labour discipline, resisting union demands, limiting 'compliance costs' to business	Need to check resource demands of public sector and 'do more with less'

Source: Adapted from Hood, 1991.

duty-bound post-war government and moved the power of trade unions and public servants into the hands of professional managers akin to doctrines one and seven (Ferlie, 2017). Through corporate governance reform, leaner executive boards would enable management by setting performance objectives rather than having them serve representative functions as expressed in doctrines one, two, three, six and seven.

Measurement reforms underscored the role of metrics in enabling management and external accountability; it was the fuel of NPM reforms as in doctrine two. Self-regulation and an emphasis on professional duties were forsaken as accountability mechanisms in favour of new regulatory (e.g., Office for Standards in Education, Children's Services and Skills (OFSTED)) and audit organisations (e.g., Audit Commission for Local Government (now defunct)). Performance management systems were built to identify poor performers using newly and systematically collected organisational data.

While NPM remains a global phenomenon, countries vary in their approach to reform. New Zealand split purchasers and providers of services into separate specialised organisations with widespread contracting out (Halligan, 2011). Sweden downsized their public service on the back of the 1990 fiscal crisis, decentralising service delivery responsibility to local governments who, in turn, looked to 'responsive' nonprofits and private firms to deliver services (Hansen, 2011).

While the UK has perhaps experimented most extensively with NPM reforms, the US is viewed as an 'idiosyncratic hybrid' combining 'pre-, non- or even anti-NPM strands' characterised by a continuation of efficiency reforms as well as anti-bureaucratic and anti-waste narratives (Ferlie, 2017, p. 8; Pollitt and Bouckaert, 2017). Instead of trying to move service delivery closer to market models as in the UK with the internal market of the NHS, US practitioners and academics emphasised the role of intraorganisational management in making public programmes more efficient. This stemmed from a fundamental belief that internal administrative processes like strategic planning, process mapping, management-by-objectives, total quality management, and performance management and budgeting were more important tools than market forces for driving improvement (Berry, 1994; Christensen and Laegreid, 2002; Gueorguieva et al., 2009; Moynihan et al., 2011; Moynihan & Kroll, 2016; Swiss, 1992).

US hybridity is observed in the federal government public management reforms of the 1990s. Led by then Vice President Al Gore, the National Performance Review (NPR) emphasised savings and downsizing – core NPM virtues – while also calling for empowerment and innovation. The NPR was in part inspired by Osborne and Gaebler's 1992 book *Reinventing Government:*

How the Entrepreneurial Spirit is Transforming the Public Sector from Schoolhouse to Statehouse, City Hall to the Pentagon. Comprised of ten principles, the book largely suggests that government can be transformed the same way that corporations were transformed: by becoming more client-focused, less bureaucratic, more flexible and innovative, and more entrepreneurial (Weiss, 1995). Despite breaking the principal-agent relationship of the legislative branch with the executive, the argument was not to reduce either's role in contemporary society but rather to fix the systems within which government workers operate, resulting in a 'smaller but stronger' organisation: governments should *eschew operational delivery in favour of oversight*, establishing 'steering organisations' that focus on system-wide leadership and policy development with enhanced monitoring and evaluation.

Despite variation in adoption globally, NPM inspired reforms changed the model of state instrumentation and intervention – supplanting direct govern*ment* for indirect govern*ance*. Marketisation through privatisation resulted in a larger move away from direct policy tools including direct spending, payments to individuals, and direct loans towards indirect policy tools such as regulation, vouchers, grants and contracts (Salamon, 2000). Savas, privatisation's greatest apostle, described it as 'changing from an arrangement with high government involvement to one with less' (1987, p. 88). In practice, privatisation is an umbrella term for the many different policy tools governments use to delegate authority, incentivise organisational effort towards policy goals, and communicate the nature of relationships with third parties. Governments decentralised and deregulated, encouraging private delivery in traditionally public sectors – including natural monopolies like water and transit. Inter-municipal cooperation and cross-sectorial partnering were also popular options as alternative or softer forms of privatisation (Alonso, Clifton and Díaz-Fuentes, 2015; Koliba et al., 2019). Governments transferred ownership via the sale of state-owned assets and enterprises. They contracted out public services to reduce state-monopoly delivery and encourage competition.

The strongest proponents of NPM were neoliberal politicians supportive of enhanced public sector efficiency and user-orientation as well as public managers either loyal to these politicians, keen to advance their bureaucratic control, or both. Its critics, meanwhile, have been individuals who oppose the blending of marketisation and managerialism on normative grounds, employees who have experienced the negative impacts of NPM, and researchers who have explored the effects of NPM and found them lacking (Torfing et al., 2020).

In truth, the effects of NPM have been largely context-dependent and difficult to generalise (Torfing et al., 2020). Nevertheless, as they have aged, NPM reforms are largely believed to have failed to make good on their glittering promises and instead have 'tended to distract middle- and upper- level officials, create massive paperwork, and produce major unintended effects' by mindlessly pushing the adoption of 'poorly grounded recipes for institutional design ... a commonly observed feature of administrative reform processes' (Hood and Peters, 2004, p. 278). Hood and Dixon's assessment of 30 years of NPM reform in the UK showed 'a darker picture of government costing substantially more and working decidedly worse' with increased running costs alongside soaring complaints and legal challenges (Hood and Dixon, 2015, 2016).

2.2 Collaboration

While NPM may have failed to deliver a government that 'worked better and cost less', it did spur significant growth in third-party providers of public goods and services (Hood and Dixon, 2015). As the number of provider organisations grew, so too did fragmentation and competition in local systems (Christens and Inzeo, 2015). This resulted in a distinct preference for partnership and collaboration from multiple sources, including 'professionals, foundations, researchers, government agencies, and groups of organizations and volunteers ... each perceive[ing] the clear need for greater communication, collaboration, and co-ordination of organizational efforts to achieve desired outcomes in local communities' (FitzGerald, Rosenbach et al., 2021 quoting Christens and Inzeo, 2015, p. 423).

In addition to reducing the formal size of government and changing the production of public services, privatisation changed the type of work being executed within public agencies (Ferlie et al., 1996). By early 2000s, the environment and practice of public management had fundamentally shifted and public managers increasingly found themselves 'facilitating and operating in multiorganizational arrangements to solve problems that cannot be solved, or solved easily, by single organisations' (O'Leary and Vij, 2012, p. 509). Governments increasingly partnered with public, private, and nonprofit organisations to implement policies, advancing the practice of collaborative public management.

In 2012, O'Leary and Vij outlined five reasons for the growth in collaborative public management practice and scholarship. First, perennial public challenges required new approaches and were larger than one organisation. Second, outsourcing – itself a 'collaborative endeavor' – had increased in 'volume and dollar amount'. Third, in pursuit of enhanced effectiveness, public officials were seeking new ways of delivering public services. Fourth, technology had enabled 'integrative and interoperable' information sharing, 'with the outcome being a greater emphasis in collaborative governance'. Fifth, citizens were seeking further engagement in governance, resulting 'in new and different forms of collaborative problem solving and decision-making' (O'Leary and Vij, 2012, p. 509).

This collaborative turn – or 'move to partner' – aligns with the emergence of New Public Governance as a public governance paradigm (NPG) (Koliba et al., 2019; Torfing et al., 2020). Unlike NPM, 'a child of neo-classical economics', NPG's intellectual roots can be found in theories from organisational sociology, institutional theory, network theory, and beyond (Osborne, 2010, p. 8). NPG assumes a plural and pluralist state characterised by inter-dependent policy-making and policy-implementing networks. Inspired by Elinor Ostrom's work on the collaborative management of common pool resources and a broader academic search for alternatives to markets and hierarchies, NPG scholarship emphasises 'the formal and informal processes through which a plethora of public and private actors formulate and achieve joint objectives through collective action' (Ansell and Torfing, 2016; Torfing et al., 2020, p. 132).

As a public governance paradigm, NPG is somewhat inchoate, concerning itself with the growth and structure of inter-organisational collaborations, the environment and constraints on collaboration, the situation and function of public managers in a network, the governance and decision-making mechanisms collaborations adopt and use, definitions of work, processes and goals, and the impact of collaborations on public policy and the policy process (O'Leary and Vij, 2012). Hence, NPG-inspired reforms typically 'stress service effectiveness and outcomes' and emphasise 'the design and evaluation of enduring inter-organizational relationships, where trust, relational capital and relational contracts act as the core governance mechanisms' rather than intra-organisational progress in competitive environments (Osborne, 2006, pp. 382, 384).

Through the establishment of co-equal ties, coalitions and networks are understood as 'the primary vehicle for pluri-centric coordination and interactive governance' (Torfing et al., 2020, p. 127). This means that at any given time, public managers 'may be simultaneously involved in managing across governmental boundaries, across organisational and sectoral boundaries, and through formal contractual obligations' (McGuire, 2006, p. 35). Conceptually, however, what constitutes collaboration is highly variable including long-term arrangements 'encouraged or prescribed by law'; formal ties within specific policy areas as with strategic suppliers; short-term informal partnerships; and even intermittent coordinative exchanges – any of which may use public contracts (McGuire, 2006, p. 35). Mandell and Steelman helpfully categorise collaboration along a spectrum where coalitions and networks are situated at either extreme. For them, coalitions are comparatively narrow in scope, participant organisations largely act in isolation, and the arrangement is likely to disband after participant organisations' tasks are finished or the problem has been resolved. Networks, meanwhile, demonstrate 'a strong commitment to multi-organizational-level goals' with interdependent ways of working, risky and extensive resource sharing, and operate indefinitely as the problems they seek to address are long-term or evolve (Mandell and Steelman, 2003; McGuire, 2006).

Networks have been identified and studied from a variety of perspectives (Molin and Masella, 2016). Networks can be thought of as both structural phenomena and vehicles for exchanging information, developing organisational capacity, and developing administrative capacity to enhance joint-working. Networks are thought to organise collective action by formally adopting 'network-level courses of action and often delivering services' (Agranoff, 2003). Literature in the network governance tradition treats networks as a mechanism of coordination distinct from hierarchy or markets whereby networks are able to produce outcomes that could not be produced by any member organisation in isolation (Provan and Kenis, 2008). Focus is thus placed on how network conditions lead to the production of network-level outcomes, including building evidence on which network structures and processes should be adopted based on measures of network effectiveness (Provan and Kenis, 2008). Consequently, network governance literature focuses on steering or orchestration activities often executed by public authorities charged with governing networks (Sørensen and Torfing, 2009).

NPM-era outsourcing fundamentally cast governments as principals and providers as agents in perpetual competition. With NPG, the role of public authorities is more so that of a steward involved in critical 'meta-governing processes' of monitoring and guiding the activities of public service contractors (Baker and Stoker, 2012, 2013). Crucially, while contractors have legal obligations – through bilateral agreements with government or as a subcontractor to government – overarching public service networks typically lack their own legal imperative. Because of this, some form of governance is necessary to ensure participants engage in collective action, that conflict is addressed, and that resources are acquired and used effectively (Provan and Kenis, 2008). Thus, the governance of public service networks has come to include strategic and operational decision-making whereby government is most commonly responsible for defining inter-organisational goals, outlining operational rules, determining membership of the network, and in some instances, retaining responsibility for network administration (Ansell and Gash, 2008; Koliba et al., 2011).

Scholars have expressed optimism and hesitance about organising the state through contracts and networks: utilising networks can be a less predictable and weaker form of social action and can complicate coordination and accountability, but at the same time networks provide greater flexibility and adaptability (Milward and Provan, 2000, p. 362; FitzGerald, Rosenbach, et al., 2021). Contrasted to privatisation – which devolves public responsibility to private actors – network-based partnership promotes shared responsibility and risk, blurring sectoral differences (Rosenau, 2000; Koliba et al., 2019). With no clear principal or agent, the accountability relationships in networks are thus recognised as being different from those found in the dyadic linkages of public contracts: networks are responsible for more than simply the sum of member organisations' contract specifications (Agranoff and McGuire, 2001). In hollow states organised through consociational arrangements structured formally by contracts and informally through relationships across levels of government and amongst stable networks of service providers, public managers are forced to shift their concerns away from organisationally determined accountability to notions of responsibility, responsiveness, and the fostering of democratic ideals: effectiveness, as 'accountability for' becomes at least as important as oversight and reporting or 'accountability to' (Agranoff and McGuire, 2001).

TPA, NPM, and NPG represent 'relatively coherent and comprehensive norms and ideas about how to govern, organize and lead the public administration' (Torfing et al., 2020). They attempt to capture government experimentation with 'policies, strategies, programmes and institutional templates that govern the particular manner in which the public sector is structured, functioning and operating' (Torfing et al., 2020). Explanations for shifts between paradigms depend on historical interpretation. A political lens suggests that paradigmatic shift is the consequence of decisions taken by political elites. An institutional lens finds that governance changes reflect widely held beliefs about what 'an appropriate way forward' looks like at a given time in a given context (Torfing et al., 2020).

A functional lens suggests that paradigms 'provide a plausible answer to specific problems and challenges that are accumulated in relation to the dominant governance paradigm' (Torfing et al., 2020, p. 152). In this way, NPM can be understood as a response to the inability of bureaucracies – both perceived and real – to respond to policy problems, including attending to economic growth. NPM can be cast as both a governance revolution promoted by neoliberals and neoconservatives trying to challenge 'central welfare state values' as well as a strategic response to fiscal stress and an attempt to preserve critical aspects of the post-war welfare state. Similar narratives could be used to explain NPG, but functionally it promotes horizontal coordination through networks and partnerships as a remedy for the dysfunctions of markets and fragmentation wrought by NPM. It likewise combats the assumption of homo economicus promoted by

NPM by re-norming value articulation as a governance mechanism and intrinsic incentive (Koliba et al., 2019; Torfing et al., 2020, p. 155).

2.3 Contracts

A sequential take on governance paradigms is a helpful organisational device, but in practice paradigmatic delineations are less clear. Governance paradigms coexist and compete, producing context-specific hybrids where authority, incentives, and values become difficult to situate within institutions and within the multilevel, multiplex networks which characterise policymaking and policy implementation today – an emerging paradigm Koliba and colleagues refer to as Governance Network Administration (GNA) (Koliba et al., 2019). Amidst this complexity, and as the preferred tool of indirect government, contracts play a hugely important role as they define what success looks like, set incentives for organisations to achieve it, and describe how parties should work together.

Despite their pre-eminence across post-bureaucratic public governance paradigms, getting contracts to 'work' remains challenging for governments. Technocratic fixes to the challenges of public contracting often focus on trying to 'complete' contracts. Because no person can design a contract which provides recourse for every eventuality faced by the parties privy to it, all contracts can be viewed as inherently incomplete (Coase, 1937; Hart, 1988; Van Slyke, 2007). Often, negative eventualities are caused by missteps in negotiating the relationship between purchasers (or principles) and suppliers (or agents). Transaction cost economics posits that the relationship between a purchaser and supplier is an 'exercise in reducing the transaction costs of negotiating and managing the relationship, while acknowledging the human characteristics of opportunism and bounded rationality' (FitzGerald et al., 2019, p. 459 referencing Williamson, 1985). Because purchasers have incomplete knowledge about suppliers, context, and the future, they cannot specify a contract which protects them from the likelihood that suppliers will behave opportunistically to boost their own profitability. For public service providers this could mean reducing costs by sacrificing quality or appropriating value by prioritising less costly populations for support (Lazzarini, 2020; FitzGerald, Tan et al., 2023).

Where purchasers are unaware of their own incomplete information and are not concerned with suppliers' self-interest, they may opt to arrange a 'general clause' contract specifying only that both parties act in good faith. Conversely, where purchasers recognise information asymmetries that may lead to suppliers taking advantage, they can endeavour to move towards comprehensive contracting. The types of contracts expected given opportunism and bounded rationality are shown in Table 2. Notably, Williamson claimed that only the lower-right quadrant 'accords with reality' (Williamson, 1985, p. 67). Because complete contracts are an impossibility, principals are in actual fact tasked with designing a 'requisite' contract, one that combats opportunism without over inflating costs (Williamson, 1985; Brown, Potoski and Van Slyke, 2018; FitzGerald et al., 2019).

The argument is that the involvement of profit-seeking private actors can be beneficial in areas where quality is more straightforwardly monitored, that is, where contracts are more easily completed. Crucially, monitoring the quality of private goods and services is very different than monitoring that of public ones. For the former, the important elements of quality have market proxies, namely price. For public goods and services, important attributes of quality are harder to contract and verify – improvements to quality of life, reductions in homelessness, optimal job placement or improved job retention. Indeed, a perennial problem in public contracting is incentivising service providers to support the full range of programmatic objectives sought by governments rather than simply progressing those which maximise profit (Lazzarini, 2020).

Efforts to complete contracts can take a variety of different forms many of which emphasise the rather technical specification of incentives through payment of enforceable commitments. Under NPM-inspired approaches, 'competition supplemented with performance measurement linked to conditional incentives' was intended to combat opportunism and provide public accountability (Torfing et al., 2020, p. 56). Consequently, contract forms associated with NPM often stipulate prices or methods of calculating payment for the delivery of services: fixed price, cost-reimbursement, cost-plus, time and materials, fee-for-service, unit price. These kinds of contracts leave governments to pay in arrears and are designed principally to control costs, provide oversight of activities, and enhance efficiency. Awarded through procurement processes designed to promote competition at the point of

Table 2 Contract types under bounded rationality and opportunism (Adapted from Williamson, 1985)

Bounded rationality→ Opportunism↓	Absent	Admitted
Absent	Bliss	General clause contracting
Admitted	Comprehensive contracting	Serious contracting difficulties

award to secure the lowest price from providers, contracts which focus on the authentication of costs and completion of activities can enable governments to drive down cost, but this can compromise quality (Shiva et al., 2024). This 'tyranny of lowest price' fundamentally increases the risk of contract failure as suppliers are incentivised to underbid with governments paying regardless of whether contracted services achieve programme objectives and overarching policy goals.

Concern about the growth of government contracting often focused on the degree to which government authority was too 'dispersed' and 'diluted' to effectively deliver accountability to the public. While early rhetoric regarding contracting out was alarmist (Salamon, 1989), later research on indirect government sought to refine key concepts and test the effects of 'changing governance configurations' on efficiency and effectiveness as well as equity of access, client responsiveness, democratic accountability (Heinrich, Lynn and Milward, 2010, p. i4).

The underperformance of early outsourcing encouraged broader experimentation with performance contracting as a way to fix poor quality issues and better align diverse public and private interests, better reflecting 'the complicated nature and "technology" of public programs' (Barnow, 2000; Heckman et al., 2011; Heinrich and Kabourek, 2019, p. 869). 'Where the 1980s had assumed contractors were greedy criminals, the 1990s recognised that most contractors are industrious resources willing to fulfil the government's need with ingenious solutions for a fair price' (Nagel, 1999, p. 508). Longer-term contracts that transferred the design and operation of public services to the private sector emerged, creating public–private partnerships across levels of government, in a range of shapes and sizes, and in a variety of policy areas, including innovation partnerships, urban development, infrastructure projects, public services, and policy partnerships (Torfing et al., 2020, p. 127). Governments likewise began designing contracts which paid on the basis of delivering outputs (e.g., a certain number of attendees at a job readiness course) rather than activities (e.g., holding three job readiness courses) as way of bolstering service effectiveness and offsetting risk (see Table 3). These early-term output incentives, however, were found to only loosely and sometimes negatively correlate with longer-term policy goals (Barnow, 2000; Schochet, Burghardt and McConnell, 2006; Heinrich and Marschke, 2010), meaning that while the amount paid by public managers would vary by level of success, a valid link between success as defined by the contract and success in terms of achieving policy goals and objectives was tentative at best.

Table 3 Public governance paradigms and contract forms (Adapted from Osborne, 2006; Koliba et al., 2019)

Paradigm	Governance Structure	Accountability	Contract Types
TPA	Public bureaucracies (*hierarchy*)	Inputs	Direct provision
NPM	Public bureaucracies OR private firms (*market*)	Activities Outputs	Fee-for-service Performance
NPG	Public bureaucracies WITH private firms, nonprofits, and citizens (*network*)	Outputs Outcomes Relationships	Performance Outcomes-based
GNA	Multilevel, multiplex governance networks (*nested networks*)	All forms	Outcomes-based Formal-relational

More recent experimentation extends the logic of performance contracting, shifting the focus from outputs to outcomes in an attempt to enhance accountability, reduce opportunism, and further improve service quality through personalisation and innovation (Bovaird and Davies, 2011; FitzGerald, Fraser and Kimmitt, 2020; FitzGerald et al., 2023a; Olson et al., 2024). Outcomes are increasingly used to promote collaboration and flexibility in service provision and frequently feature in how public bodies are assessed, as definitions of success, as mechanisms for collaboratively designing and prioritising interventions, in deciding who and how to contract with partners, and to incentivise interdependent activity during delivery (Bovaird and Davies, 2011). There exists an array of outcomes-oriented reforms in public contracting, each distinguished by 'a financial logic' meant to 'shape decisions about how to invest public, philanthropic and financial capital in social programmes in deference to expectations about the kinds of returns that can be expected' (FitzGerald et al., 2023a, p. 331).

Outcomes-orientation has four major categories relevant to public contracting. First, *outcomes-oriented funding* evaluates service provider performance using outcomes but does not explicitly tie the achievement of outcomes to payment as in results-driven contracting (e.g., European Social Fund). Second, *outcomes-based funding* as in OBC evaluates service provider performance using outcomes and does explicitly tie the achievement of outcomes to payment as in payment-by-results (e.g., UK Work Programme, UK Troubled

Families, USAID Financing Ghanaian Agriculture Project). Third, *investor-backed OBC* where payment is contingent upon outcomes achievement *and* investors cover the up-front costs of service delivery as in social outcomes contracts (SOCs) – also known as social impact bonds (SIBs), development impact bonds, social benefit bonds, or pay-for-success (PfS) initiatives (FitzGerald et al., 2023a). Fourth, where outcomes are *additional* to the primary policy objective of a contract. Called 'collateral policies' (Cibinic & Nash, 1998), 'buying social justice' (McCrudden, 2007), 'horizontal policies' (Arrowsmith, 2010), 'buying social' (EC, 2011), and 'social value' (UK Cabinet Office, 2021), these outcomes feature as additional elements which are built into public contracts to pursue wider economic, social, or environmental policy goals (as in sustainable or green public procurement). These additional outcomes can feature in any public contract, including health and social care, and articulate, for example, explicit preference to contract with small or local businesses, for suppliers to report and minimise carbon emissions, requirements of non-discrimination in employment, or preference for bids which advance job creation.

Crucially, the use of outcomes aligns with a general shift from technocratic to relational mechanisms for completing contracts whereby outcomes are both extrinsic incentives and frameworks to enable collective action amongst service providers. Even as governments have moved to collaborate, their reliance on contracts has not abetted for important reasons explored in Section 3. New ways of contracting have been explored which deemphasise transactional dynamics between purchasers and suppliers in favour of relational mechanisms. While shades of relationalism feature in long-standing contract theories in the form of probity and trust, attempts to design governance mechanisms which advance or accelerate such elements are fairly recent. Applied work on public contracting has thus transitioned from suggesting technocratic remedies for one-off contracts between government and a single provider to describing how contracts might inform ongoing partnerships between governments and provider consortiums by outlining dynamic governance mechanisms that foreground the enabling role of trust between parties. Echoing lessons from collaborative governance and governance network literature, some scholars have noted and called for more 'braiding' of formal and information contract mechanisms (Gilson, Sabel and Scott, 2010), framed by others as 'formal relational contracting' (Frydlinger, Hart and Vitasek, 2019). While the focus of relational contracting was initially on private contracting, there are more recent expressions of hope that relational contracting approaches will improve public contracting for social outcomes (Carter and Ball, 2021; Gibson, 2023).

3 Public Procurement

We have so far emphasised the political, economic, and managerial dimensions of public contracting. Our conversation on contract specification has thus been informed by theories of incomplete contracts, transaction cost economics, and relationalism, driven by attempts to understand how governments might design contracts and collaborations to boost performance as increasingly measured by the social outcomes they deliver.

In this section, we turn to the legal basis of public contracting by exploring the duties of public procurement professionals and the rules they operate within. Managerialism and legalism are considered distinct and often conflicting intellectual approaches to public management (Christensen, Goerdel and Nicholson-Crotty, 2011; Rosenbloom, Kravchuk and Clerkin, 2022). Managerialism foregrounds the importance of balancing conflicting values of efficiency and performance. Legalism, meanwhile, emphasises a balance between discretion, innovation, and accountability through legal priorities and processes (Christensen, Goerdel and Nicholson-Crotty, 2011). Scholars have argued that the tension between law and management 'has grown significantly more visible,' with the 'market-based reforms of new public management' favouring efficiency and performance 'to an even greater degree relative to legal and democratic mores such as accountability, equality, transparency, representativeness, and value plurality' (Christensen, Goerdel and Nicholson-Crotty, 2011, p. i125).

Within the academic debate, public law has been characterised as both an essential champion of democratic values and an 'unwarranted constraint on the effective implementation of public programs' (Christensen et al., 2011). As it relates to public contracting, scholars have long argued that private provision raises the possibility that democratic values are ignored (Domberger and Jensen, 1997; Brown, Potoski and Van Slyke, 2006), with early studies showing that programme recipients in contracted out welfare services 'enjoy fewer due process protections' with worsening accountability (Bezdek, 2000; Diller, 2001; Christensen, Goerdel and Nicholson-Crotty, 2011). Still, there are those who suggest that an overly legalistic view inherently undervalues privatisation because it seeks to constrain 'the private role in public governance' rather than working to 'facilitate and direct it' (Freeman, 2000; Christensen, Goerdel and Nicholson-Crotty, 2011).

We suggest, as others have, that contemporary public management combines managerialism and legalism with a focus on efficiency and performance as well as the values expressed in public law – 'increasing representation, facilitating citizen participation, and building collaborative relationships that ensure value plurality in the administrative process' (Christensen, Goerdel and Nicholson-Crotty, 2011, p i132). We likewise advance the notion that public procurement professionals are expected to deploy a combination of legal *and* managerial skills to ensure that public contracts are well-implemented, high-performing, and reflective of democratic values.

In this section, we first discuss public procurement professionals as specialised public managers charged with unique duties and skills that are beyond those required in other sectors. For example, we expect public procurement professionals to translate and implement broad public policy aims through relatively narrow and short-term public contracts while being transparent and accountable to political oversight bodies, competing businesses, and civil society. The discussion of public procurement professionals as specialised public managers details the international movement to professionalise public procurement by increasing discretion and developing competencies that blend the public policy and business elements of their role. This section highlights the risk that limiting this professional role to the setting and approval of outcomes payments reduces the focus on wider issues of public integrity, public standards, and public policy aspects of public service delivery.

We then turn to the public law rules that constrict or dilate what can be done on any public contract. These can include international trade, anticorruption, and competition rules and regulations as well as further rules that implement policy priorities of the applicable legislative body. We describe three layers of rules within which public procurement professionals must operate: overarching procurement principles, the contracting organisation's wider policies, and transaction-level rules. This section also highlights the challenges that OBC can introduce.

Finally, we address tensions in the shift towards the public procurement of outcomes within OBC whereby changes to contract forms can frustrate the standard use of contract templates and implied terms, especially when the role of the government is limited to approving a fixed payment for achievement of an outcome. Here, we use a logic model framework to differentiate the commitments found in standard procurements with those expressed in OBCs to underscore those elements of a contract that government staff is likely to find difficult or impossible to give up in pursuing outcomes – especially in a social programme supporting vulnerable or protected populations.

3.1 Specialised Public Managers

Public procurement professionals are specialised public managers charged with awarding and managing government contracts. As noted by the OECD, public procurement is 'recognised as a strategic instrument for achieving government policy goals aligned with the 2030 Agenda for Sustainable Development, including promoting a circular and green economy, stimulating innovation, supporting small and medium-sized enterprises, and promoting ethical behaviour and responsible business conduct' (OECD, 2023, p. 6). In the US, Europe, and elsewhere, these public managers have a wide range of discretion in the expenditure of huge sums of public money and the delivery of essential public services. This discretion includes contract design – selecting the right contract type or a blend of contracts, considering issues of pricing, risk, and incentives – and then working with contractors throughout contract performance.

In the US federal procurement system, a highly specialised public manager role is prescribed in regulations – along with subordinate functions to which some authority is delegated. The authority to 'enter into, administer, or terminate' a government contract is given only to the role of 'Contracting Officers' (FAR Subsection 1.602-1). The Federal Acquisition Regulation (FAR) also provides that '[c]ontracting officers are responsible for ensuring performance of all necessary actions for effective contracting, ensuring compliance with the terms of the contract, *and safeguarding the interests of the United States in its contractual relationships*. To perform these responsibilities, Contracting Officers should be allowed *wide latitude to exercise business judgment*' (FAR Subsection 1.602-2 Responsibilities). The Contracting Officer has an important discretionary role when making any contract award. The FAR provides that contracts can only be awarded to 'responsive prospective contractors' and that, after the procurement procedure and before the award of a contract, the Contracting Officer must make 'an affirmative determination of [contractor] responsibility' (FAR Section 9.103). The Contracting Officer must thereby determine that the prospective contractor meets various standards, including 'a satisfactory record of integrity and business ethics' (FAR Subsection 9.104-1). For contract management and administration, the Contracting Officer delegates authority to a Contracting Officer's Representative (COR), who must be trained and experienced, but the authority to make changes to the contract is not delegated to the COR (FAR 1.602-2).

The structure size of the procurement workforce in the US government has received regular attention from the US Congress, including through various commissions, legislation, and numerous reports from the US Government Accountability Office (GAO). Examples include the President's Blue-Ribbon Commission on Defense Management (the Packard Commission) in the 1980s, the Defense Acquisition Workforce Improvement Act in the early 1990s, and related reforms established acquisition career paths for military and civilian personnel and a Defence Acquisition University. The strengthening of individual managers at the level of contracting entities and the contract was clearly framed as consistent with the then President Regan's distrust of government and the quest to be more like the private sector. The Chairman, David Packard (co-founder of computer giant Hewlett-Packard or HP), noted in his foreword to the report:

> *Innovations in American industrial management, yielding products of ever higher quality and lower cost, have provided a key insight: human effort must be channeled to good purpose through sound centralized policies, but free expression of people's energy, enthusiasm, and creativity must be encouraged in highly differentiated settings. ... Excellence in defense management will not and can not emerge by legislation or directive. Excellence requires the opposite – responsibility and authority placed firmly in the hands of those at the working level, who have knowledge and enthusiasm for the tasks at hand.* (President's Blue Ribbon Commission on Defense Management, 1986, xi–xii)

The EU, meanwhile, does not prescribe roles in the Procurement Directive – this is a matter for member states. Nonetheless, the European Commission has taken steps to clarify and strengthen public procurement roles, including the publication in 2020 of a 'European competency framework for public buyers (ProcurCompEU)' pursuant to the 2017 adoption of 'Recommendation on the professionalisation of public procurement as one of the priorities of EU public procurement strategy' (European Commission, 2017, 2020). The ProcureComEU materials summarise practical challenges in public procurement, namely that it is 'not a clearly defined organisational function with a corresponding training, recruitment and career path' and is 'frequently conducted as an additional task by civil servants that may lack specific procurement-related skills'. Furthermore, 'business-related skills are often underrated in the public administration resulting in an overly legalistic, compliance-focused approach' (European Commission, 2020, p. 12). In ProcureCompEU, public contracting activities and responsibilities are described and structured in thirty competencies divided into procurement-specific competencies and soft competencies. Many of these competencies might feature in any private sector organisation, but some highlight the public nature of the role. Perhaps the clearest example is 'Competence 3, Legislation,' which provides:

> *Public procurement professionals need to understand and be able to apply the relevant national and EU level legal frameworks and the principles of non-discrimination, equal treatment, transparency, proportionality and sound financial management. This includes adjacent areas of law and policy, e.g.: Competition, administrative, contract, environmental, social and labour laws, accessibility obligations and Intellectual Property Rights; EU funding, budgetary and accounting rules; Remedies; Anti-corruption and anti-fraud measures; Any relevant international obligations.* (European Commission, 2020, p. 34)

There has been a long trend in growing the discretion of public managers involved in public procurement. To address problems in US government procurement of computing technology in the 1980s, Steve Kelman called for greater public manager discretion, suggesting that its absence 'extracted a terrible cost in the poorer performance of contractors selling computer systems to the government (and in other areas of procurement as well)' (Kelman, 1990). At the turn of the millennium, Sue Arrowsmith noted a trend in the UK, US, and other states towards more discretion rather than detailed legally enforceable transparency requirements (Arrowsmith and Trybus, 2002). However, the 'right' amount of discretion and transparency around procurement remains unclear. For instance, recent quantitative studies based in Europe find that discretion is associated with the section of politically connected firms (Szucs, 2023), especially by less transparent public authorities (Baltrunaite et al., 2021). Similarly, research has found that discretion is associated with more frequent awards to the same organisations, although this does not necessarily negatively affect procurement (Coviello et al., 2017).

The ongoing international movement to professionalise public procurement is focused on more discretionary and strategic functions rather than administrative functions. Professionalisation includes setting certification and training standards to encourage the development of competencies that blend the public policy and business elements of the role. Reforms related to the training of public managers in the procurement workforce have continued through the present day and the priorities of different administrations have been reflected. This is illustrated by a recent (2023) White House memorandum on the 'Federal Acquisition Certification in Contracting (FAC-C) Modernization', which states:

> *Contracting professionals are the most important part of the Federal acquisition system. Their training and development are critical to the success of important public priorities, such as advancing equity, promoting sustainability, increasing domestic sourcing, and ensuring our supply chains and cyber assets are secure. ... Today's professionals are highly trained and skilled in exercising business judgment, being innovative, and gaining efficiencies, all while being effective stewards of taxpayer dollars.* (Office of Management and Budget, 2023, p. 1)

The reference to equity in the memorandum above is consistent with an executive order issued by President Biden in 2021 on his first day in office, titled Advancing Racial Equity and Support for Underserved Communities Through the Federal Government (Office of Management and Budget, 2021, Executive Order 13985). This executive order specifically references public procurement and required agency heads to submit a plan for addressing 'any barriers to full and equal participation in agency procurement and contracting opportunities'.

3.2 Procurement Rules

The specialised duties and skills expected of public procurement professionals are conveyed across three layers of rules, as expressed in Table 4: overarching procurement principles; ties to wider economic, social, and environmental policy goals; and rules directly related to the transaction or collaboration.

Furthest from the transaction, overarching procurement principles embody commitments to public values like transparency, integrity, and competition (Schooner, 2011, 2002). These principles are evident in international trade and international development, including anticorruption mechanisms and the strengthening of national and local public financial management systems. For example, twenty-one parties are subject to the World Trade Organisation's Government Procurement Agreement (GPA), including the US, EU, and UK (with the EU's twenty-seven countries counted as one party). The GPA includes commitments regarding non-discrimination and the conduct of procurement. Another example is found in the Model Law on Public Procurement adopted by the United Nations Commission on International Trade Law (UNCITRAL), which reflects international procurement best practices that balance efficiency and performance alongside legal and democratic values of accountability, transparency, fairness, and equality (Yukins and Nicholas, 2023). The preamble describes objectives:

> *(a) Maximizing economy and efficiency in procurement; (b) Fostering and encouraging participation in procurement proceedings by suppliers and contractors regardless of nationality, thereby promoting international trade; (c) Promoting competition among suppliers and contractors for the supply of the subject matter of the procurement; (d) Providing for the fair, equal and equitable treatment of all suppliers and contractors; (e) Promoting the integrity of, and fairness and public confidence in, the procurement process; (f) Achieving transparency in the procedures relating to procurement.* (UNCITRAL, 2011)

Significantly, these overarching principles do not focus on getting the lowest price, suggesting that the role of the modern procurement professional is more about getting value and effectiveness from contractors than pushing them to lower prices. The EU's Procurement Directive provides that awards will be based on the most economically advantageous tender, often referred to as 'MEAT', and this 'shall be identified on the basis of the price or cost, using a cost-effectiveness approach ... and may include the best price-quality ratio, which shall be assessed on the basis of criteria, including qualitative, environmental and/or social aspects, linked to the subject-matter of the public contract in question' (EU Directive 2014/24, Article 67). In the US, FAR provides

Table 4 Three layers of procurement rules

Layer	Description	Examples
3. Overarching principles	Frequently expressed in international rules and development initiatives, as well as national and sub-national rules	• Competition / non-discrimination, integrity, and transparency principles in WTO Government Procurement Agreement 2012 • UNCITRAL Model Law on Public Procurement 2011
2. Wider economic, social, and environmental policy goals	Increasingly integrated into procurement via social value, community well-being, equity policies	• UK's National Procurement Policy Statement (2021) • Scotland's 'Sustainable procurement duty' in legislation (2014) • US White House Executive Order on 'Catalyzing Clean Energy Industries and Jobs Through Federal Sustainability' (2021)
1. Transaction or collaboration related	Contractual terms and public procurement regulations implied and/or incorporated into the contract by law	• Inherently Governmental Functions (FAR 7.7) • Change Clauses in US Federal rules (FAR 43) • Limitations to amendments in EU Procurement Directive (Directive 2014/24/EU, Article 72)
Public manager with a specialised procurement function managing public contracts		

a commonly used process for negotiating contracts to achieve the best value and allows the Contracting Officer to 'trade-off' cost and non-cost factors, such as the quality of the approach or past performance.

The middle layer of rules relates to leveraging public spending through government contracts to help achieve wider economic, social, and environmental goals. Issues of effectiveness and equity in areas such as sustainability and local economic development are being considered at the point of contract award and during contract delivery (Schooner and Speidel, 2020). Akin to the fourth form of outcomes-orientation outlined in Section 2, these rules often allow for the inclusion of outcomes that are additional to the primary policy objective of a contract. For instance, a government contractor engaged to build a school may also be required to report carbon emissions during construction, commit to hiring local apprentices to work on the project, or engage small businesses or social enterprises.

McCrudden labels attempts to tie policy goals and contracting policy as 'procurement linkages' exemplified in disabled workers' rights after the Second World War as well as civil rights and anti-discrimination laws in the US, Europe, Canada, and Australia resulting in selective purchasing and boycotts for different categories of business (e.g., 'set-asides' in the US) (McCrudden, 2007). In the UK, the practice of implementing wider economic, social, and/or environmental policies through public contracts is labelled 'social value' by the Public Services (Social Value) Act 2012 and is advanced by various Public Procurement Notices (PPNs). Social value is also promoted in the current UK National Procurement Policy Statement, a publication that now has a legal basis in the UK's new Procurement Act (2023). The Statement provides: 'All contracting authorities should consider the following national priority outcomes alongside any additional local priorities in their procurement activities: creating new businesses, new jobs and new skills; tackling climate change and reducing waste, and improving supplier diversity, innovation and resilience' (UK Cabinet Office, 2021, p. 3). The various UK social value policy statements provide a similarly broad framework with a wide range of policies that may be included in any public procurement (Cabinet Office, 2021). In Scotland, the Procurement Reform (Scotland) Act 2014 creates a sustainability duty and requirements to include 'community benefits' in contracts over a certain threshold or provide an explanation of why these are not applicable.

Crucially, this category of outcomes orientation is growing – especially in green public procurement and the pursuit of carbon emission targets (i.e., Net Zero goals) through government contracts (Schooner, 2021; Dimand and Cheng, 2023; Janssen and Caranta, 2023). In the UK, PPN 06/21 requires contractors over a certain size to produce Carbon Reduction Plans setting out how the organisation intends to achieve 'net zero' carbon emissions by the year 2050. The US now has a 'Buy Clean Initiative' and recently proposed a new rule for the FAR that would require Federal contractors (over certain sizes) to disclose emissions, disclose climate-related financial risk, and set targets to reduce greenhouse gas emissions (US Gov, 2022). The EU also has developed various materials and tools to support green public procurement. Notably, the pursuit of Net Zero goals is not only a top-down policy issue. The 2015 Paris Agreement shifted carbon reduction from being a regulatory issue to a multilateral issue for many levels of subnational government and non-state actors (Hale, 2016). This means that in addition to national-level targets, many contracting authorities have their own Net Zero targets and many try to implement these targets through their own contract spending. As climate change challenges grow, this area is likely to continue growing at all levels of government. Notably, concerns have been raised about accountability and the extent to which social value policy choices within contracts meaningfully reflect the priorities of nationally and locally elected offices or legislative bodies (Davies, Buys and Macdonald, 2023).

Finally, public procurement professionals are constrained and enfranchised by terms within contracts as well as rules which stipulate how to enter and amend contracts. In a private contract, parties can focus on each other and their commitments to each other. Generally, they are the only party who can enforce those commitments. In contrast, external actors have a greater role in public contracts as they may dispute the award or performance of the contract based on failure of the public contracting authority to follow public law rules. Likewise, depending on the jurisdiction, other public law bodies may be involved in enforcing or monitoring the implementation of public law rules. The public nature of the contract can also limit the flexibility the parties have to change the contract. Changes in governmental requirements are often privileged above those of private parties. This privilege constitutes another source of risk for contractors and can undermine the ability of both parties to remain committed to firm prices longer term, especially over periods of volatility. Unlike a contract between private parties, where the parties can easily arrive at a new agreement and amend their contract, public parties must also consider whether the change requires a new procurement altogether.

The FAR provides detailed standard clauses for US government contracts which impact contract management, including clauses to make changes relatively easy for the government. In the US federal procurement system, the FAR gives the Contracting Officer significant power to unilaterally change the public contract and the contractor will have to comply (FAR Part 43). If an agreement about adjusting the contractor's price cannot be reached, the contractor will be paid for the change based on their costs. In terms of any contracts involving a fixed price for outcome, this may mean that a change to the outcome may change the contract from fixed price to costs (i.e., from paying for an outcome to paying for inputs and activities). However, while the government's power to make unilateral changes is very wide, it is not unlimited – US courts have decided the government cannot make a 'cardinal change' that would be a 'drastic modification' beyond the scope of the contract, though this will differ under circumstances of a specific contract (e.g., see US Court of Federal Claim decision in *Air–A–Plane Corp.* v. *United States*, 187 Ct.Cl. 269, 408 F.2d 1030, (1969)).

The EU's Directive does not try to provide standard clauses for the contracts – this is for member states' own contracting rules – but does provide some limitations on the changes that can be made. This area of public contracting has been called 'dark side of EU procurement law' due to the lack of transparency and research in the performance of government contracts when compared to the award of government contracts (Dragos et al., 2023 p. 1). The 2014 Directive does not give the relevant public manager this unilateral power. The EU Directive does provide for modification of contracts during their term (Article 72), under various circumstances, including the provision for amendments in the original published documents or changes that do not modify the contract for 50 per cent of the value of the original contract (Article 72). The European Court of Justice has emphasised that these changes cannot make the contract 'materially different' from the contract described in procurement notices.

3.3 Contract Design

At the nexus of the three layers of public rules described, public procurement professionals exercise their discretion directly in the award, design, and management of public contracts (Davies, 2008). A central design consideration is the type of government contract awarded categorised according to the way that the enforceable commitments are priced. In the US, the FAR provides definitions and detailed clauses for different types of contracts, including fixed price contracts (i.e., payment as a predetermined value for services provided), cost reimbursement contracts (i.e., payment as allowable incurred costs of service provider), and time and material contracts (i.e., payment based on time and materials spent by service providers to fulfil agreed scope of work) – any of which may have a performance incentive element (See FAR Part 16). In the EU, the 2014 Directive does not provide such detail but leaves this up to member states. For example, the UK's model services agreement provides for different pricing mechanisms, including fixed price contracts, time and materials, volume pricing, and a cost-based pricing called Guaranteed Maximum Price with Target Cost.

In the US, the selection of contract type is at the discretion of the Contracting Officer as a matter of 'negotiation and requires the exercise of sound judgement' (FAR 16.103). The FAR provides considerations for selecting contract types that are helpful for understanding incentives and encourage a blended approach or evolving blend of contract type during the course of service delivery and performance. For instance, an acquisition programme or even a contract may go through 'changing circumstances' where a different type of contract becomes appropriate in later periods than was used at the outset of the project (FAR 16.103-4). According to regulations, fixed price contracts are more suitable for less complex and less 'governmental' contracts:

> *Complex requirements, particularly those unique to the Government, usually result in greater risk assumption by the Government. This is especially true for complex research and development contracts when performance uncertainties or the likelihood of changes makes it difficult to estimate performance costs in advance. As a requirement recurs or as quantity production begins, the cost risk should shift to the contractor, and a fixed-price contract should be considered.* (FAR, 16.104)

In essence, the skill of public procurement professionals lies in their ability to specify and price enforceable commitments as well as articulate how their delivery will be verified. Fundamental to OBC is that the definitive enforceable commitment of the contractor will occur further into the delivery period than is traditionally the case. To illustrate this point, we use a generic logic model which represents the presumed path of converting resources into activities which generate priority outputs and outcomes. Historically, public contracts have worked to specify inputs and activities presumed to lead to outputs and outcomes. With OBC, the emphasis of those enforceable commitments shifts to the right – and a purely outcomes-based approach would effectively include a fixed price for outcomes – but in practice, a mix is often used (see Table 5 for further detail on enforceable commitments).

Inputs that the government may need to make enforceable in the contract include personnel and facilities involved in contract performance. For example, the government may consider that the qualifications or experience of key personnel is an important criterion for awarding the contract and wants to approve key personnel changes. Similarly, the government may require that personnel working with vulnerable people have security clearance or background checks and that facilities meet relevant industry standards, all of which may be subject to change. For some *activities*, the government may need to

Table 5 Enforceable commitments of contractor

	Input	Activity	Output	Outcome
Programme logic	Financial, human, and other resources mobilised to support activities	Work performed to convert inputs into specific goods and services	Near-term results from converting inputs into activities	Positive results in the lives of recipients Objectives of the programme
Enforceable commitment examples	Personnel or subcontractor qualifications Facility standards Accounting system	Complying with labour policies, accounting standards, carbon emission reduction reporting, etc. Submitting personnel or subcontractor qualifications for approval if making changes after award Following a process for enrolling people into or excluding people from the programme Participating in meetings, complaints mechanism, etc. Participating in monitoring, evaluation, and/or learning activities	Progress reports Structured data on key performance indicators	Specified outcome(s)

require contractor compliance with a wide range of rules regarding safe workplaces, fair employment rules, environmental practices, accounting standards, anticorruption measures, conflict of interest rules, subcontracting rules, and beyond. More directly related to the programme, the government may want participation in regular monitoring meetings, a role in deciding who is eligible or ineligible for (or otherwise excluded from) programme participation, and a role in resolving complaints or emergency situations. The government may also need the contractor to participate in an evaluation or other third-party procedures to validate the achievement of enforceable commitments, especially outcomes. Meanwhile, contractors may also want enforceable terms around the government's role in promoting or referring people into the social programme so that the outcomes can be achieved. *Outputs* that the government may need during the programme's activities include periodic information on progress towards outcomes, whether as regular updates or detailed data to monitor progress or to comply with public information rules. The government may also want to understand *how* outcomes are being achieved and to secure learning outputs, technical guides, or other programme documents.

Still, as we describe in Section 4, the promises of OBC are principally advanced by tinkering with only one aspect of the contractual form: the enforceable commitment. The tension between a simple contract document that focuses on outcomes and a more complex contract that incorporates other rules is highly salient in outcomes contracting, and beyond. Practitioner advocates of outcomes contracts have emphasised that an outcomes contract should focus on fixed prices for the outcomes and avoid over specification of inputs or activities (Government Outcomes Lab, 2019). However, public rules compel public procurement professionals to further specify inputs, activities, and outputs so that they might discharge their duties rooted in the advancement of democratic values. This means that the contracts which structure outcomes-based contracts (OBCs) also require clauses about how human resources are to be managed, corruption is to be avoided, environmental sustainability is to be advanced, safety is to be ensured, and vulnerable populations are to be protected.

4 Outcomes-Based Contracting

Heralded as a mechanism to drive solutions to some of the most complex and expensive social problems, OBC emphasises monetised social outcomes to guide public service implementation and oversight amongst novel, intersectoral partnerships that coordinate the funding, management, and service provision (Roberts, 2013; Carter, 2021, p. 79; FitzGerald et al., 2023a). As an approach which bundles multiple modern public service reforms – public–private partnerships, performance management, evidence-based policymaking, and outcomes-orientation (Heinrich and Kabourek, 2019) – OBC has proliferated over the past decade to include a host of differently branded contract and collaboration approaches, including results-based finance, pay-for-performance, payment-by-results, PfS, SOCs, SIBs, social outcomes partnerships (SOPs), social benefit bonds, and beyond. Key areas of variation in OBC include the degree to which payment is tied to long-term outcomes and whether external private investment is leveraged to cover the upfront costs of service delivery as in SIBs – now more commonly called SOCs or SOPs (Carter, 2020; FitzGerald et al., 2023).

By positioning outcomes as the key enforceable commitment in public contracts, OBCs promise to mitigate two perennial challenges in public service contracting. First, a focus on measuring and managing shared outcomes is meant to help bring entities together, advancing coordinated holistic support for individuals beyond what any one organisation could achieve in isolation. In services for vulnerable populations, the interdependencies and need for well-orchestrated collective action is heightened as these cohorts require an array of health and human services which are delivered by several organisations (Johnston and Romzek, 2008; Carter et al., 2024). Second, OBC attempts to address the problematic aspects of incompleteness in public contracts to moderate the ill effects of opportunistic providers and enhance public accountability (Lazzarini, 2022). Viewed through transaction-cost economics, the use of longer-term outcome measures validated by robust evaluation methods can be viewed as an attempt to 'complete' the contract.

The nature of OBC conveys that outsourcing decisions do not simply end with contract award. Instead, public procurement professionals are tasked with determining how to design and manage service contracts over time and in partnership with multiple actors, suggesting that the procurement task at hand is to weight the costs and benefits of contracting in a particular way (Shiva et al., 2024). When designed well, OBC offers assurance to policymakers and public managers that the public services delivered today generate the positive outcomes of tomorrow. By specifying outcomes, OBC is geared at improving the links between policy design and policy implementation, representing what Peters calls a 'deliberate endeavour to link policy tools with clearly articulated policy goals ... based on the systematic effort to analyse the impacts of policy instruments on policy targets' (Peters et al., 2018, p. 4). By expanding monitoring functions and situating robust evaluation methods within the payment mechanisms of contracts, OBCs can de-risk government spending, incentivise collective action, and build evidence on 'what works' in complex health and human services (Carter et al., 2018; Lazzarini, 2022).

OBCs require public procurement professionals to contractualise the who, what, and when aspects of policy targets – the treatment cohort, the expected outcomes of the intervention, and the period over which outcomes can be achieved. OBCs also include elements of policy calibration by identifying implementing agencies and their roles, for example, as service providers, project managers, funders, and evaluators. In addition, OBC often stipulates monitoring and accountability rules designed to course correct underperformance during contract delivery (FitzGerald et al., 2021; Ronicle, Stanworth and Wooldridge, 2022; Howlett, Ramesh and Capano, 2023). By design, OBC makes explicit the micro-level policy components that calibrate macro-level public governance paradigms and meso-level policy tool preferences for implementation. OBC attempts to align general goals and governance approaches at the macro-level with meso-level programmatic objectives and tools and micro-level incentive schemes and management routines all while creating a strategically flexible operational environment (Peters et al., 2018; Howlett, Ramesh and Capano, 2023, p. 5). In such a way, outcomes can be thought of as a mechanism for establishing a 'golden thread' between macro-level policy goals and micro-level policy specifications in a public service environment characterised by networks.

Public governance paradigms occur at the macro-level, and public contracting is an embedded meso-level policy tool within those paradigms. Meso-level work commonly features studies of the interplay between governance capacities enacted through policy tools and instruments such as subsidy, regulation, contracting (Hood, 1986; Salamon, 2000; Hood and Margetts, 2007). It is widely recognised that scholarship has addressed the macro- and meso-level components of public policies – paradigms, governance arrangements, objectives and tools – but significant shortcomings exist related to micro-level components, where policy goals, programmes, and instruments are implemented in the form of 'policy targets and tool calibrations', as expressed in Table 6 (Cashore and Howlett, 2007; Howlett, Ramesh and Capano, 2022). Howlett, Ramesh, and Capano suggest that 'a key challenge to real-world policy making is determining how to match policy goals with the means available to implement them' (Howlett, Ramesh and Capano, 2023, p. 1).

As the evidence on OBCs shows, these targets and calibrations are of critical importance: as macro-level policy goals expressed in governance paradigms become operationalised for implementation through public procurement, their internal mechanisms for change can decouple at the meso- and micro-level (Torfing et al., 2020; Howlett, Ramesh and Capano, 2023). When this happens, the quality of implementation can suffer, the efficacy of interventions can be eroded, unintended effects can emerge, and failure can be more likely – as when

Table 6 Policy components (Cashore and Howlett, 2007; Howlett, Ramesh and Capano, 2023)

		Focus		
		Sectoral (macro) Level	**Programme (meso) Level**	**Specific Measures (micro) Level**
Content	**Aims**	**Policy goals** What general types of ideas govern policy?	**Programme objectives** What does policy formally aim to address?	**Policy targets (specifications)** What are the on-the-ground requirements of policy?
	Instruments (means)	**Instrument logic** What general instrumental principles guide policy?	**Policy instrument choices** What specific types of instruments are utilised?	**Design of instrument package (calibrations)** Ways of delivery of instruments?

OBCs maximise payment to suppliers but leave policy problems unaddressed (FitzGerald, Tan et al., 2023; Hevenstone et al., 2023).

OBCs, particularly SOCs, merge NPM narratives of market discipline, privatisation, and managerialism with the collaborative and relational narratives associated with NPG (Heinrich and Kabourek, 2019; Fraser, Knoll and Hevenstone, 2022; French et al., 2022; FitzGerald et al., 2023). In blending marketisation thorugh contracting, managerialism in pursuing outcomes, measurement through validating attributable outcomes, and relationalism by enabling partnership working, proponents suggest that OBCs can simultaneously balance the managerial values of efficiency and performance with the legal requirement of accountability (Christensen, Goerdel and Nicholson-Crotty, 2011; Mulgan et al., 2011; FitzGerald, Tan et al., 2023). By this logic, outcomes allow governments to provide strategic direction to service providers and promote innovation and flexibility at the frontline, at once aligning 'financial incentives and social goals' to improve cross-sector collaboration and ultimately outcomes for service users. Accountability is likewise ensured as governments notionally do not pay for services unless they generate valid outcomes.

In the US and UK, forms of OBCs – namely SOCs and PfS – have targeted multiply disadvantaged cohorts who experience several touch points with the state, including homeless individuals trying to secure housing alongside substance misuse treatment and enrolment into entitlement programmes (e.g., Santa Clara County Project Welcome Home); older people whose loneliness is causing health problems and placing unnecessary burden on primary and urgent care facilities (e.g., Worcester Reconnections); and families with children at risk of being taken into foster care in need of therapeutic support (e.g., Oklahoma Intensive Safety Services). In both national contexts, private and nonprofit providers are prevalent, delivering specialised services under an array of disjointed, bilateral public contracts overseen by different units within and across governments. Where people require multiple services paid for by multiple government departments, 'synergies and connections across the ultimate objectives of provision are difficult to manage' … resulting in support gaps for services users, duplication of effort, and individuals being 'buffeted between several different agencies or service providers' (Carter et al., 2018, p. 10).

OBC frequently attempts to pull these parties together. While they can vary greatly in partner form, OBCs minimally involve a party that pays for outcomes and a party that delivers services. Depending on the complexity of the project, OBCs may also include a party that verifies the achievement of outcomes to trigger payment and a party that manages the day-to-day operations of the project – this can be either an intermediary or a prime contractor. In SOCs, there is also a party that provides up-front investment capital to cover the costs of service delivery. In UK SOCs, the outcomes payer is almost always government, the service provider is typically a nonprofit, the project manager is often aligned with investors, and the capital comes from socially motivated private investors. UK SOCs do not often include an independent evaluator to validate outcomes. Instead, that role is frequently left to government who pays based on administrative data or self-reported data from project partners, usually the project manager. In the US, project managers are more likely to be independent from investors, the evaluators are more likely to be present and tasked with running at least quasi-experimental evaluations to validate outcomes and trigger payment, and the capital comes from a blend of philanthropic and institutional investors alike (Economy, Carter and Airoldi, 2022).

SOCs, in particular, have been the subject of very polarised debate, with an optimistic 'narrative of promise' promoting them as the solution to a lack of public sector innovation and entrepreneurship, and a 'narrative of caution' where through financialisation, they advance investor profit seeking over public and voluntary efforts. (Warner, 2013; Lake, 2015; Fraser et al., 2018; Tse and Warner, 2020b). The supposed benefits of the SOC model of OBC are multitudinous. They purport to 'enhance innovation at the front-line due to increased freedom to providers brough about by a focus on outcomes' (Gustafsson-Wright, Gardiner and Putcha, 2015); 'transfer risk to the private sector by placing new services upstream of negative social outcomes without government having to pay for both prevention and crises services simultaneously' (Gustafsson-Wright, Gardiner and Putcha, 2015); 'scale promising social interventions' (Kohli et al., 2012); 'spur collaboration across levels of government and between service-providing organizations by creating a mechanism for pooling resources toward outcomes rather than service streams' (Roman et al., 2014); 'yield cashable savings for the public sector' (Liebman and Sellman, 2013); and 'diversify the public service supply chain by enabling smaller and voluntary sector organizations to take on government contracts, particularly payment-by-results contracts, as investors bear performance risks' (HM Government, 2012; FitzGerald et al. 2020, pp 87–88).

After over a decade of experimentation, however, and despite promises of improved collaboration and service quality, it remains unclear whether OBC and SOCs are more effective than other policy instruments for delivering public services (Dayson, Fraser and Lowe, 2020; Hajer and Loxley, 2021). Some have argued that the NPM-inspired performance management routines of SOCs have actually damaged partner relationships as compared to traditionally financed projects (Dayson, Fraser and Lowe, 2020) and that SOCs increase costs, creating 'pecuniary advantage' to their lead stakeholders, 'potentially at the expense of the broader public interest' (Hajer, 2020). Studies have also shown that very few SOCs have 'delivered broader system changes' chiefly because they do not attempt to alter the behaviour of 'powerful actors that create societal and market failures that cause social problems' (Tse and Warner, 2020a). Tse and Warner's analysis of thirteen SIBs in early childhood services shows that even when projects endeavour to target meso-level institutions, they pay for micro-level outcomes, 'applying market discipline to weaker actors like public institutions and vulnerable clientele' (FitzGerald, Fraser and Kimmit, 2020, p. 93 referencing Tse and Warner, 2020a). Critics suggest that it is precisely the process of operationalising outcomes into enforceable commitments within contracts that forces a shift towards narrow, financialised concepts of social value (Tse and Warner, 2020a, 2020b; Golka, 2022).

This means that purchasers in OBC have a difficult balance to strike. With outcomes as a critical enforceable commitment in the contract, the 'traditional routes of completing a contract are less applicable: purchasers cannot simultaneously dictate a detailed means of delivery and then insist on holding suppliers responsible for the outcomes those requirements produce' (FitzGerald, Tan et al., 2023, p. 1799). The task for purchasers is then to specify outcomes such that they curtail opportunism while allowing for flexibility. In OBC, opportunism broadly comes in two forms. Suppliers can economise on non-contractible service elements (i.e., reduce costs) or they can focus on more profitable service users (i.e., cherry-pick, cream, or park) (FitzGerald, Tan et al., 2023).

Given the heterogeneous nature of social service cohorts supported by OBCs and the possibility of service providers and investors behaving opportunistically, ideal-type outcomes specifications (or 'requisite' contracts (FitzGerald et al., 2019)) are those that incentivise providers to 'support all programme participants effectively considering their differing support costs and varied likelihoods of realizing specified social outcomes and thus triggering payment', and constrain providers' ability to 'appropriate economic rents' while retaining OBC's perceived benefits of flexibility and relational working (FitzGerald, Tan et al., 2023, p. 1797 referencing Newhouse, 1984, van de Ven and van Vliet, 1992; Carter and Whitworth, 2015).

Guidance on the specification of outcomes in SOCs suggests that to mitigate the ill effects of supplier opportunism, purchasers should include (i) clear eligibility criteria for cohorts; (ii) outcomes that are logically and empirically linked to overarching policy goals; and (iii) an estimate of deadweight in the outcomes price (FitzGerald et al., 2019; FitzGerald, Tan et al., 2023). To prevent suppliers from prioritising more profitable subpopulations at the point of referral (i.e., cherry-pick), contracts should include mechanisms which protect independence in the referral process. This could mean identifying a treatment cohort using independently held data, setting up neutral third-party referral boards, or arranging for post-referral audits. To prevent suppliers from prioritising more profitable subpopulations within the referred cohort (i.e., creaming-and-parking), purchasers could undertake advanced population segmentation to identify and personalise support offers ex ante or differentiate payment, stipulate minimum service requirements, or implement caps on the number of payable outcomes by type. To ensure that payable outcomes demarcate meaningful changes in the lives of service users, public managers should select outcomes measures which are conceptually aligned to overarching policy and represent causally valid improvement. This suggests minimal use of shorter-term activity or outcome payments which are sometimes negotiated into OBCs to rebalance risk across stakeholders. Finally, on deadweight estimates, including a method of ensuring attribution of outcomes to contracted services prevents public managers from paying for outcomes which could have occurred without the OBC (i.e., comparing performance against the so-called counterfactual). This means estimating deadweight through the inclusion of a counterfactual within the payment mechanism: an expression of what could or would have happened in the absence of OBC provision. From less to more robust methods, this could include benchmarked self-reported data, baselined administrative data, or even quasi-experimental or experimental impact evaluations with statistically estimated treatment effects (FitzGerald et al., 2019; FitzGerald, Fraser and Kimmitt, 2020; FitzGerald et al., 2023).

Consider the world's first SOC, SIB at the time, launched in 2010 at Her Majesty's Prison Peterborough. Designed by the UK Ministry of Justice in consultation with Social Finance UK, a nonprofit intermediary organisation (and subsequent programme manager), the SIB sought to reduce reoffending amongst a cohort of 3,000 short-term prisoners over a six-year period. Using a network of differently specialised nonprofit organisations, the SIB offered wrap-around support to individuals leading up to and after their release from prison, including accommodation, substance misuse, job training, family support, and benefits and financial advice. Ten different investor organisations provided up-front capital to fund services, and if re-convictions fell by more than 7.5 per cent across the cohort over the life of the project, validated by an independently executed quasi-experimental impact evaluation, their principle would be repaid plus a return. In 2017, after some changes to the project specification due to broader shifts in probation services within the sector, the 7.5 per cent reduction was achieved and the Ministry of Justice released outcomes payments but did not pay out at the maximum possible contracted value (Disley et al., 2016; Anders and Dorsett, 2017; FitzGerald et al., 2019; FitzGerald, Tan et al., 2023).

In other words, recommended routes for specifying outcomes include enforceable commitments tied to inputs (e.g., mandating external evaluation or credentialled personnel to make service referrals), activities (e.g., defining referral processes or requiring data sharing and participation in learning and evaluation), as well as outcomes. In Peterborough, the referred cohort was tightly defined and everyone eligible was referred although participation was voluntary. The payable outcome was likewise directly proximate to the policy objective – payment for reductions in reconvictions as a proxy for reoffending. Finally, a real-time deadweight estimate in the form of an externally executed impact evaluation featuring propensity-score-matched national sample comparison group meant that outcomes payments were for reductions in reconvictions over and above what would have occurred in the absence of the service (FitzGerald et al., 2019).

4.1 UK Outcomes Funds

We can explore further attempts to align policy design and implementation using OBC in two UK outcomes funds: the Department for Work and Pensions (DWP) Innovation Fund and the Department for Digital Culture Media and Sport (DCMS) Life Chances Fund.

Outcomes funds are formal processes for developing, approving, and funding multiple and simultaneous OBCs (Savell et al., 2022). Outcomes funds have been integral in solidifying the UK's pre-eminence in OBCs globally, quickening the development of the social investment market and driving up the number of OBCs, particularly SOCs, domestically. The UK is home to 98 of the world's 288 SOCs, 91 of which have been at least partially supported by an outcomes fund. Collectively, UK SOCs deliver a range of health and human services to over 116,000 individuals primarily in England (INDIGO, 2023).

Outside of the UK, outcomes funds are active in Africa with the 2018 establishment of the Education Outcomes Fund for Africa and the Middle East now active in Sierra Leone and Ghana as well as two outcomes funds in South Africa: the 2020 South Africa Green Outcomes Fund and the 2023 Jobs Boost Outcomes Fund; in Australia with the 2022 New South Wales Social Impact Outcomes Fund ($30 million (ASD) available for outcomes payments); in Latin America with the Logra Outcomes Fund in Colombia (Col$ 17.56 billion available for outcomes payments); and in Europe with Portugal Inovação Social (€15 million), the Dutch Brabant Outcomes Fund (€1 million), and two French outcomes funds: Economie circulaire (€10 million) and Egalité des chances économiques (€10 million) (Savell et al., 2022; INDIGO, 2023). In the US, the 2018 Social Impact Partnerships to Pay for Results Act passed through Congress, allocating up to $100 million USD for outcomes payments validated through independent experimental or quasi-experimental methods (Savell et al., 2022). Outcomes-based contracts are being increasingly launched in lower- and middle-income countries and are increasingly considered by international development agencies and financial institutions when they contract international development interventions (Elsby et al., 2022).

One of the defining features of the UK SOC market is the role of central government, especially the 2010–2015 Conservative coalition government, which took up SOCs as a way to off-set austerity cuts in the wake of the global financial crisis by crowding in new forms of investment to the social sector (Williams, 2020). In 2012, UK central government focused their efforts on building the supply side of the SOC market, establishing a pipeline of social investment capital from dormant bank accounts through the creation of Big Society Capital, a social investment wholesaler who has since seeded three SOC investment funds managed by Big Issue Invest and Bridges Fund Management (Williams, 2020, p. 8). To build the demand side of the social investment market, UK central government has designed and launched ten outcomes funds, committing over £220 million to outcomes payments (Savell et al., 2022).

Generally, outcomes funds follow four key stages. The first is an initial designation of outcomes funding by one or more public, private, or philanthropic organisations. This designation of funding is often also publicised with set overarching objectives which might include the targeted number of OBCs to be supported, priority outcome areas, and indicative metrics for use in outcomes validation. The second phase is a call for proposals or invitation to tender where service providers, investors, intermediaries, public actors, and even pre-established partnerships are invited to submit bids in the hope of securing funding for outcomes which align with the articulated aims (e.g., supporting priority cohorts, promoting activity in specific policy areas) and means (e.g., agreeable outcomes prices, inclusion of essential stakeholders (i.e., co-funders of outcomes, investors, or evaluators), and participation in the outcomes verification process this is a floating) of the fund. The third phase involves an adjudication of bids by the funders or their agents. Where the outcomes funder is government, selection at this stage will likely kick off a more formal public procurement contract award process to formalise and mobilise the partnership. The final phase includes executing the process of validating and paying for outcomes as ascribed by the outcomes fund (Savell et al., 2022).

4.1.1 The Innovation Fund

The world's first outcomes fund, the Innovation Fund, was led by the UK central government DWP. Part of a £60 million support package to improve outcomes for young people aged fourteen to twenty-four years who were or were at risk of becoming not in employment, education, or training (NEET), the Innovation Fund made £30 million available to provide support to SIBs (as they were then called) to test the effectiveness of social investment models for this cohort (Savell et al., 2022). The DWP expressed three overarching policy objectives for the Fund: (1) to deliver support to young people and improve their employability; (2) to test whether cashable savings can be realised alongside other fiscal and social benefits; and (3) to develop the social investment market, the capacity of smaller delivery organisations, and the evidence base for social investment arrangements. To structure the fund, the DWP set out general eligibility criteria and outcomes specifications based on a rate card included in the invitation to tender (see Table 7). On the back of this, SIB partnerships – which could include local authorities – were invited to submit bids to the DWP over two procurement rounds. The first, in April of 2012, resulted in six SIBs. The second round, in November of the same year, resulted in four.

In these bids, SIB-providers tendered for targeted numbers of outcomes at specified unit prices. In the bid specification and application documentation for

Table 7 DWP Innovation Fund rate card (Adapted from Griffiths, Thomas and Pemberton, 2016)

Outcome Measure	Maximum Price of Outcome	
	Round I	Round II
Improved attitude towards school/education	n/a	£700
Improved school attendance	£1,300	£1,400
Improved school behaviour	£800	£1,300
QCF-accredited entry-level qualification	n/a	£900
Basic skills	n/a	£900
First Level 1 NQF qualification	£700	£1,100
First Level 2 NQF qualification	£2,200	£3,300
First Level 3 NQF qualification	£3,300	£5,100
First Level 4 NQF qualification	£2,000	n/a
English for speakers of other languages	£1,200	n/a
Entry into first employment (thirteen weeks)	£2,600	£3,500
Entry into first employment (twenty-six weeks)	£1,000	£2,000
Cap per individual young person	£8,200	£11,700

each round, the DWP outlined its maximum willingness to pay for particular social outcomes, allowing SIB-providers to define their intervention model, referral criteria, numbers, and mechanisms, and their preferred mix of outcomes at discounted unit prices from the rate card. The DWP did cap the total amount payable to SIB-providers on each project using the sum of the tendered number of outcomes multiplied by their unit prices (the 'contract cap') with the maximum amount payable per individual set first at £8,200 in round one and then climbing to £11,700 in round two. Policy documents have suggested that these individual payment caps were derived from three years of annually managed expenditure savings per capita – the value of avoided job seekers allowance for each individual (DWP, 2012; Griffiths, Thomas and Pemberton, 2016; Thomas, Griffiths and Pemberton, 2016). All ten projects ran for three years, with outcomes monitored for an additional six months. To trigger payment from DWP, projects self-reported their achievement of outcomes using administrative data (FitzGerald et al., 2019).

4.1.2 The Life Chances Fund

Announced in 2016 as an £80 million Outcomes Fund, the UK central government Department for Digital, Culture, Media and Sport (DCMS) Life Chances Fund made three rounds of funding available across six themes: drug and alcohol dependency, children's services, young people, early years, healthy lives, and older people's services. Applicants with proposals outside of these themes could still be considered for Life Chances Fund funding if proposals proved innovative, well-designed, and good value-for-money (UK DCMS, 2016). In policy documents, DCMS expressed the overarching aim of the Life Chances Fund as 'help[ing] people in society who face the most significant barriers to leading happy and productive lives' (UK DCMS, 2016, p. 1) but articulated seven objectives which would enable this to occur:

> *i) increasing the number and scale of SOCs in England; ii) making it easier and quicker to set up a SOC; iii) generating public sector efficiencies by delivering better outcomes and using this to understand how cashable savings are; iv) increasing social innovation and building a clear evidence base of what works; v) increasing the amount of capital available to a wider range of voluntary, community and social enterprise (VCSE) sector providers to enable them to compete for public sector contracts; vi) providing better evidence of the effectiveness of the SOC mechanism and the savings that are being accrued; vii) growing the scale of the social investment market* (Cabinet Office, 2016, p. 1).

To structure the fund, DCMS opted for a locally led funding model, where the £80 million Life Chances Fund envelope is used to pay for a percentage of the outcomes specified in and delivered via local procurement. In policy documents this top-up is capped at less than 50 per cent of the outcomes payments for any individual project, with a goal to average top-up payments at 20 per cent for the Fund overall. The Life Chances Fund did not stipulate particular interventions to be commissioned nor did it set out a rate card. Application materials did, however, outline what kinds of projects would be given preference for funding. Since the Life Chances Fund aimed to scale the size and number of SOCs, the articulated preference was for bids that '(i) improve or re-align provision, (ii) co-ordinate multiple stakeholders to tackle complex issues, (iii) scale to unlock future savings and (iv) seek innovative solutions' (Cabinet Office, 2016, p. 2). Beyond that, to receive Life Chances Fund funding, bids had to demonstrate that a local commissioner(s) was committed to paying for measurable outcomes which would not be covered by the Life Chances Fund in a deal that was capable of attracting external social investment (UK DCMS 2016). There was also a general requirement for local evaluation to be undertaken but that evaluation did not have to feature in the payment mechanism.

The design of the Life Chances Fund supported local actors – local authority commissioners and/or service providers – to develop projects. The process for this started with a call for expressions of interest from projects. Expressions of interest were then screened by TNLCF, who were hired by DCMS to administer the Fund. Any bids that met these criteria were invited to submit a full application and, if additional financial support was required for technical expertise to develop the proposal (e.g., financial modelling, service and outcomes definition, and theory of change), apply for a development grant, a small pool of money available in addition to the £80 million allocated for outcomes payments. Upon completing a full application, bids were then reviewed by an expert panel who made in-principle decisions on which bids would receive funding. The Life Chances Fund also included non-pecuniary support for applicants delivered by TNLCF, the newly launched academic research centre and official evaluator of the Fund, the Government Outcomes Lab (GO Lab) at the University of Oxford, and Traverse, a consultancy group. During the early stages of the Life Chances Fund, these delivery partners offered guidance to applicants on procurement, contract design, evaluation, and stakeholder management.

At the conclusion of the applications process, thirty-one SOCs received Life Chances Fund funding representing six policy areas: child and family welfare (ten), employment and training (eight), health and well-being (five), homelessness (four), education and early years (three), and criminal justice (one). Local governments then moved to procure and contract services for their SOCs. In this regard, the Life Chances Fund did not attempt to limit local discretion, simply stating:

> *We expect your contracting arrangements to offer good value for money, selecting any new providers through open procurement involving consideration of at least three potential suppliers. Use of pre-qualification questionnaires, drawing from a pool of experienced potential suppliers, Voluntary Ex-Ante Transparency (VEAT) notices and similar arrangements are all acceptable provided they are compliant with the commissioner's financial standing orders and national contract law.* (FitzGerald, Hameed et al., 2021, p. 27 quoting UK DCMS, 2016)

In practice, Life Chances Fund contractors used a variety of procedures, but evaluation material suggests that they varied widely in their ability to use flexibilities afforded to them in law, whereby in some areas the procurement process was 'a very process-oriented, risk-averse function' (FitzGerald, Hameed et al., 2021, p. 28). Local procurement procedures were cited as an 'important source of significant cost and frustration' for LCF [Life Chances Fund] applicants with the 'novelty of commissioning outcomes, and the involvement of investors mean[ing] that standard market engagement and procurement procedures were not always fit-for-purpose' (FitzGerald, Hameed et al., 2021, p. 11).

4.2 Discussion

As policies, the Innovation Fund and the Life Chances Fund are consistent at the macro- and meso-levels. Broadly, they seek to improve outcomes for people while saving or avoiding costs. They also aim to build the social investment market by boosting the capacity of actors within that market to participate in OBC, *and* they attempt to create evidence on the efficacy of OBC particularly SOCs. They prescribe cross-sector partnerships involving investors structured via OBCs. At the micro-level, however, they convey considerable variance in policy targets and calibrations seemingly driven by diverging approaches to the level of discretion granted to project partners.

In the Innovation Fund, the DWP maintained direct discretion over policy targets and calibrations through the rate card, defining the core policy issue, providing outcomes definitions, and calculating maximum prices. The Fund also provided clear direction as to the process through which projects are expected to evidence their outcomes for payment. While local actors still assumed responsibility for fulfilling bid requirements, the design complexities of identifying and prioritising the service cohort, defining payable outcomes and providing for their validation, and securing additional outcomes funding do not feature. The Life Chances Fund does nearly the exact opposite by delegating substantial discretion to local actors. In setting up the Fund, DCMS provided very general guidelines around priority service cohorts and outcome definitions by identifying thematic policy areas and stipulating that bidders must evidence how cost savings accrue. In the absence of greater specification centrally, local actors were given the discretion to identify and prioritise service cohorts and viable interventions in addition to contractualising outcomes capable of accruing savings to local *and* central governments. Local governments are likewise left to procure and contract their projects as well as validate outcomes achievement through whatever means they see fit.

Neither the Innovation Fund nor the Life Chances Fund prescribe intervention models nor referral pathways, allowing projects to determine their mechanisms for connecting individuals to contracted services. In the Innovation Fund, the logic of the rate card presumes progression from improved behaviour to further qualifications and employment, but in practice projects were paid for any mix of outcomes subject only to an individual cap on total outcomes payments (DWP, 2012, p. 15). In the Life Chances Fund, these particularities are instead negotiated on a project-by-project basis, with deviations from submitted project plans addressed through discussion with TCLF, DCMS, and project partners. Where a project undertakes a major amendment, there is a formal approval process, but limited information is available publicly on the nature of these changes. While project performance data is being released on Life Chances Fund projects, wide variation in the definitions of payable outcomes prevents comparative analysis across projects like that undertaken on projects in the Innovation Fund. External evaluation does not feature in the payment mechanisms of Innovation Fund nor Life Chances Fund projects. Instead, payment is based on the submission of predetermined administrative data by local actors that is further scrutinised by the DWP directly or by TNLCF on behalf of DCMS (see Table 8).

The Innovation Fund somewhat reduced capacity requirements on local actors by specifying the rate card and eligibility criteria. While local actors still assume responsibility for preparing bid documents and fulfilling requirements set by central government during delivery, for example project monitoring, the complexities of identifying and prioritising a service cohort and payable outcomes as well as negotiating who pays for those outcomes locally is not required of projects. The Life Chances Fund increases capacity requirements for local actors as they are left to specify and calibrate SOCs in accordance with the policy objectives of central government as well as engage with a more complex stakeholder network, including other project partners – fellow outcomes payors, providers, intermediaries, and investors – as well as the delivery partnership of the Fund – DCMS, GO Lab, TNLCF, and Traverse. Affiliative network maps (see Figures 1 and 2) visualise the contractual relationships galvanised by each outcomes fund. Funded SOC projects are indicated by blue circles which are scaled according to the financial size. Lines represent membership in projects

Table 8 Comparing the Innovation Fund and the Life Chances Fund

	Innovation Fund	**Life Chances Fund**
Identifies the policy issue and eligible cohort	Central government in policy strategy and eligibility criteria for participating cohort in bid guidance	Local government and/or providers identify policy issue and cohort that may appeal to sponsoring body
Defines outcomes	Central government in rate card	Local government in conversation with other actors
Prices outcomes	Central government in rate card	Local government in conversation with other actors
Leads procurement	Central government	Local government
Validates outcomes	Central government	Local government
Pays for outcomes	Central government	Local government pays majority with 'top-up' from central government
Commissions evaluation	Central government	Central and local government

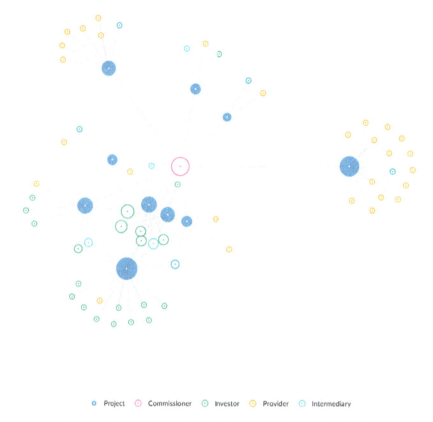

Figure 1 DWP Innovation Fund network. (INDIGO, 2023).

and member organisations are represented by circles colour coded according to their function: pink circles indicate outcomes payors, yellow circles indicate service providers, green circles indicate investors, and teal circles indicate intermediary organisations. Member circles are scaled according to the number of projects in which they participate, hence the pink circle in the centre of each network represents central government – DWP in the Innovation Fund and DCMS in the Life Chances Fund. The result of granting greater discretion to local actors to design projects and bring in additional outcomes payors is a larger and denser network in the Life Chances Fund. For DCMS, this means needing to manage relationships and provide oversight to a greater number of projects and project partners to ensure that the fund-level collaboration makes progress towards their overarching fund-level objectives.

In terms of delivering against stated policy objectives (as in Table 9), the picture is somewhat mixed. Innovation Fund did deliver support to young people, test the evidence base for social investment and its ability to generate cashable

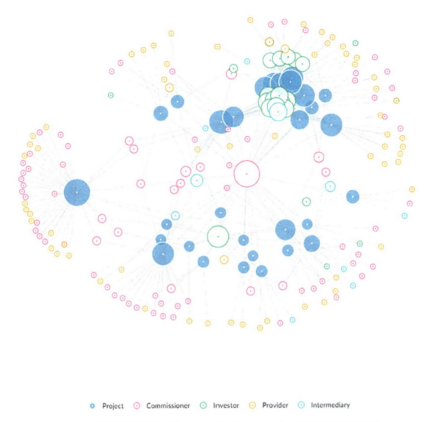

Figure 2 DCMS Life Chances Fund network. (INDIGO, 2023).

savings, and helped to develop the social investment market. For longer-term objectives, however, the Fund does not deliver. Employment opportunities for participating young people did not improve, and while the fund did test whether social investment generated savings and improved outcomes, the results were not favourable: the benefits of social investment were not outweighed by the costs involved in designing and managing Innovation Fund projects according to the impact evaluation (Salis, Wishart and McKay, 2018).

Interim qualitative evaluation of the Innovation Fund highlighted that most projects experienced delays in the initial stages of implementation, reducing the number of referrals and intervention starters, and consequently resulting in a remodelling and re-profiling of targeted outcomes. With this remodelling, initial intervention differences between projects diminished, resulting in a more uniform focus on younger age groups, on working within schools, and offering more time-limited interventions. Thus, projects identified as performing the 'best' in the early stages of the fund were those that targeted pre-NEET young

Table 9 Assessment of policy objective achievement in the Innovation Fund

Policy Objective	Achieved	Comment
To deliver support to young people and improve their employability	No	Ten projects delivered services to young people (YPs). In the main, however, outcomes for YPs supported by the Fund were not better, and in some instances were worse, than YPs who did not receive support
To test whether cashable savings can be realised alongside other fiscal and social benefits	No	Social return on investment analysis included in evaluation showed a negative SROI ratio due to the negative impact evaluation results, meaning benefits did not outweigh costs
To develop the social investment market, the capacity of smaller delivery organisations, and the evidence base for social investment arrangements	Mixed	The Innovation Fund more than doubled amount of UK SIBs at time of launch. The evaluation material does not directly address ongoing capacity within participating delivery organisations but subsequent SOCs have included the same stakeholders, suggesting these ways of working have been developed by some partners within the Fund. Department for Work and Pensions commissioned qualitative and impact evaluations are important touch points in the development of the evidence base of UK SIBs. Findings do not support wholesale application of social investment models

people through schools, included a high number of intermediate or shorter-term outcomes, had a rolling and sufficiently large intake of referrals, and providing differentiated but time-limited support to young people (Griffiths, Thomas and Pemberton, 2016).

The final qualitative evaluation of the Innovation Fund showed that all parties perceived the projects to 'have been a great success, with targeted numbers of outcomes met or exceeded' and most agreed that 'projects had achieved better results than they would have done if commissioned using more traditional methods' (Griffiths et al., 2016; Thomas et al., 2016, p. 1). Participating young people described experiencing 'changes in their attitudes and approach to issues in their lives; improvements in social and familial relationships; and a broadening of their employment and career horizons' (Thomas et al., 2016, p. 3). The final quantitative evaluation – executed solely to generate evidence rather than trigger payment – was not so positive (Salis, Wishart and McKay, 2018; De Pieri, Chiodo and Gerli, 2022). Findings of the quasi-experimental impact evaluation showed that Innovation Fund participants aged fourteen to eighteen were less likely to be in education and employment than those in the comparator group, while more were in training; that fourteen- to fifteen-year-old participants were less likely to achieve NQF level 2 and 3 qualifications than young people in the comparator group; and that fourteen- to fifteen-year-old participants were more likely to be truant or experience school exclusion. Overall, the Fund was not shown to achieve value-for-money as many of the outcomes would have been achieved regardless (Salis et al., 2018). As 'projects realised that projected numbers of outcomes per young person would be lower than anticipated', they increased recruitment, with the 'numbers of discreet outcomes achieved per young person' often being 'quite low'. The time frame of the programme also meant that longer-term employment and education outcomes were all but abandoned by some projects (Griffiths, Thomas and Pemberton, 2016, p. 40). The outcomes specification choices set out by DWP meant that projects could overrefer easier-to-treat individuals into support services and then generate payment by overdelivering on earlier-term output measures at the expense of longer-term outcomes (FitzGerald et al., 2023). Recent analysis from across the Innovation Fund shows that outcomes payments in eight of the ten funded projects hit their maximum contracted value with returns paid to investors.

For the Life Chances Fund, the full picture of performance is not yet known as some projects are contracted to pay for outcomes into 2026 (see Table 10). The Covid-19 pandemic also created substantial complications for projects, forcing some to deviate from their pre-specified outcomes, others to completely change their method and scope of service delivery, some to delay their launch, and a small number to terminate (FitzGerald, Hameed et al., 2021). While

Table 10 Assessment of policy objective achievement in the Life Chances Fund

Policy Objective	Achieved	Comment
Help people in society who face the most significant barriers to leading happy and productive lives	Mixed	While support is being offered, the long-term effects will not be known until projects complete delivery and final outcomes payments are made. Because local actors have specified outcomes, a standard assessment for performance across the fund is not readily available
Increasing the number and scale of SIBs in England	Mixed	LCF funding has resulted in thirty-one additional SIBs in England, but the median size of projects remains below £1 million within the UK
Making it easier and quicker to set up a SIB	No	Evaluations suggest that funded projects struggled to design, procure, and mobilise projects. Complications with Covid-19 caused further complications and delays
Generating public sector efficiencies by delivering better outcomes and using this to understand how cashable savings are	–	Too soon to tell
Increasing social innovation and building a clear evidence base of what works	Mixed	The variation across projects in chosen cohorts, interventions, and payable outcomes means the evidence generated from projects is unlikely to contribute to a generalisable body of knowledge about successful support approaches
Increasing the amount of capital available to a wider range of voluntary, community, and social enterprise (VCSE) sector providers to enable them to compete for public sector contracts	–	Too soon to tell
Growing the scale of the social investment market	–	Too soon to tell

support is being offered to service users, a detailed account of how well each funded project performs against its initial and renegotiated payable outcomes will be required to comment on whether the Fund has supported individuals to lead happy and productive lives. The lack of standardised outcome measures as in the Innovation Fund rate card or minimum required evaluation approaches embedded into project payment mechanisms likewise means that assessing overall fund performance will remain challenging. While projects are delivering support to individuals throughout England, the degree to which that support will lead to durable improved outcomes will be challenging to assess even once final outcomes payments have been made.

5 Conclusion

After their experience with the Innovation Fund, the DWP improved their rate card, tweaking it for use in two subsequent outcomes funds: the Youth Engagement Fund and the Fair Chance Fund. They specifically bore down on defining referral pathways so as to mitigate the potential for cherry-picking and included caps on outcome types such that providers could not cream-and-park users in order to overdeliver on earlier-term metrics at the expense of longer-term outcomes. Published evaluation material falls short of making strong attributional claims about the benefits of both funds but does highlight an improved balance between outcomes delivered and financial reward (ICF, 2019; Ronicle and Smith, 2020; FitzGerald et al., 2023b).

As we have argued in this Element, so much of the success or failure of public contracts is determined by the skill with which their enforceable commitments are negotiated and defined. Now over a decade into experimentation, the evidence on OBC suggests that the degree to which they allow governments to pay for outcomes of questionable value is significantly dilated or constrained by how they are specified, with careful consideration needed for how cohorts are identified and connected to services, how well evidenced and firm the links between payable outcomes and long-term policy objectives are, and how integrated counterfactual thinking is in pricing (FitzGerald et al., 2019; FitzGerald, Tan et al., 2023).

On the one hand, outcomes orientation is consistent with a more strategic role for public procurement by granting an expanded pool of professionals the discretion to concretely operationalise public policy aims through public contracts. On the other hand, practically or even notionally reducing the role of the government in contract management to simply approving outcomes payments clashes with the legal obligations of public procurement professionals to protect the public interest throughout contract performance. As such, outcomes are at once a solution to and embodiment of the managerial and legal tensions within public administration as they promise to enhance efficiency and performance as well as buttress public duties when contracting for service delivery. Even with careful specification, however, doing the business of government through outcomes carries inherent risk, especially when the business in question includes the outsourcing of complicated and essential services.

In this concluding section, we distil the risks and challenges of OBC in two ways. First, we suggest that governments may lack the necessary capacity to succeed at the procurement and management of OBC, and as such, use it as a way of contracting-out their responsibility for regular involvement in outsourced provision. Second, we highlight that OBC may enable governments to circumvent their legal duties of accountability and reviewability as a way of contracting out their liability. We then close with a brief commentary on the continued necessity of government involvement in contracted services, even those guided by social outcomes.

5.1 Contracting Responsibility

On a public management level, it may be tempting to think of OBC as an opportunity to set outcomes, find a contractor or a team of contractors, agree on a price, and let folks 'get on with it'. This may be even more tempting if the agency adopting such a 'set-and-forget' model has limited capacity to perform the management that might be required in more traditional contracting. But there is little evidence to suggest that OBCs require less capacity than other contracts to manage. On the contrary, the inclusion of wider policy outcomes in contracts and management approaches likely requires *more* capacity. Outcomes take time to set and may need careful revision during delivery. This is especially the case for high-powered incentive contracts like SOCs that require significantly more time to procure and attention to manage than other types of contracts (FitzGerald et al., 2019). Simultaneously, the task of public procurement is increasingly a more complex strategic function for government as it is seen to be an important lever for achieving public policy goals with a wide range of economic, environmental, and social outcomes being included in public contracts. This, combined with the realities of getting public contracts to deliver in increasingly networked and dynamic social programme environments, likely means that *more* involvement of procurement professionals is needed during contract performance.

In the US, there has been both a push towards performance incentives and a realisation of the importance of capacity in procurement. In the US, Congress recently established the independent Advisory Panel on Streamlining and

Codifying Acquisition Regulations (the Section 809 Panel), which highlighted that the 'DoD's acquisition workforce is the lynchpin to achieving successful acquisition reform' and made recommendations focusing on the hiring, training, development, and retention of the acquisition workforce, precisely those public managers who are responsible for procurement and contract management (Section 809 Panel, 2019, p. 15). In the UK, there has been reduction in public procurement staff in the public sector overall, but an increase in the staff in Crown Commercial Services (CCS). This serves to underscore the effect of hollowing out procurement and contracting capacity particularly in UK local governments.

> *In recent years, the UK's procurement workforce has experienced two cross-cutting trends. On the one hand, the austerity policy put in place in the aftermath of the economic crisis has resulted in significant headcount reduction across government agencies, including in their procurement departments. Between 2010 and 2012, the number fell 17% from approximately 3,900 to 3,200, although over the same period, the number of staff holding Chartered Institute of Purchasing and Supply (CIPS) qualifications has increased. At the same time, the move toward greater centralisation in the CCS is increasing the professionalisation of procurement.* (European Commission, 2016, p. 223)

In the EU, the European Commission has a 'Public Procurement Action Plan' that includes a 2016 'stock-taking study' on member state's administrative capacity in public procurement. This study articulated four areas of administrative capacity: 'human resources dedicated to procurement, training and capacity building structures that ensure the proper qualification of procurement practitioners, trainings offered to procurement practitioners and economic operators, and existing systems and tools aimed at improving the way procurements are handled' (European Commission, 2016). The study found low levels of participation in skills trainings on topics such as green public procurement and social public procurement, with the cost or lack of funding being the greatest barrier to attendance.

From an oversight and monitoring perspective, beyond personnel bandwidth, the system in place for capturing and tracking contract performance and delivery of outcomes as enforceable commitments remains underengineered, particularly in the UK. Ongoing performance data for OBCs to guide day-to-day operations is often held by project managers rather than civil servants and can differ from reported key performance indicators – and indeed outcomes – across projects. As it relates to social value, the transparency notices that are required under EU directives and current UK regulations are designed to describe the core requirements of a procurement, but do not capture horizonal or collateral requirements. There is no systematic reporting or comprehensive public data on social value priorities, requirements, contracted commitments, or implementation. Without an effort to capture and publish the achievement of social value clauses, we will have no way of knowing whether the specifications and calibrations in contracts relate to the successful delivery of social outcomes.

5.2 Contracting Liability

There is also the risk that contracting authorities may outsource outcomes to avoid directly making decisions or performing activities that subject them to being accountable to democratic representatives or are reviewable by courts at the request of service users and other members of the public. In other words, authorities may view outcomes as a way to contract liability. Public authorities have duties related to public services, including those services that have been contracted out. This is a matter of concern in individual situations but is also as a wider constitutional issue. As explained by Davies: 'Public Law is not just concerned with the outcomes of cases. It is also concerned with the allocation of public powers and duties. This reflects its role in 'constituting' government. Contractualisation gives rise to difficulties in this regard because public powers or duties which are allocated to the government by statute may be exercised or performed by contractors' (Davies, 2008).

In the UK, public authorities have a wide range of legal duties. A guide to lawful decision-making for UK local authorities describes duties to declare interests, follow correct procedures, engage in consultations, stay within remit, be rational and evidence-based, include all relevant considerations, act with proper purpose, comply with the European Convention of Human Rights, be proportionate, and properly reasoned (Smith and PracticalLawPublicSector, 2022). However, it is not always clear whether an entity is a public authority exercising a public function giving rise to public duties.

In the 2003 *Aston Cantlow* case, the House of Lords (the highest court in UK at that time) was considering 'publicness' under the Human Rights Act and the European Convention of Human Rights. It emphasised that there was 'no single test of universal application' and provided some factors to be considered when assessing when public duties arose: 'the extent to which in carrying out the relevant function the body is publicly funded or is exercising statutory powers, or is taking the place of central government or local authorities, or is providing a public service' (Lord Nicholls of Birkenhead in Aston Cantlow and Wilmcote with Billesley Parochial Church Council v Wallbank [2003] UKHL 37).

However, even when it established that a contracting authority has a public duty, it is not aways the case in the UK that a contractor performing the service under a public contract will also have the duty. Duties do not automatically extend to contractors. Their extension depends on factors laid out by Court of Appeal in the *Donoghue* case (regarding homelessness), applied again by Court of Appeal in *Leonard Cheshire* (regarding elderly care, where there was no public duty applied to the contractor). Both these cases were cited favourably by the House of Lords in *Aston Cantlow*.

In the *Donoghue* case, Donoghue argued that a housing association, Poplar, had a particular duty because Poplar was a contractor to a public authority, Tower Hamlets council. The Court of Appeal found that Polar *did* have the duty. The Court of Appeal also stated:

> *66. It is desirable to step back and look at the situation as a whole. As is the position on applications for judicial review, there is no clear demarcation line which can be drawn between public and private bodies and functions. In a borderline case, such as this, the decision is very much one of fact and degree. Taking into account all the circumstances, we have come to the conclusion that while activities of housing associations need not involve the performance of public functions in this case, in providing accommodation for the defendant and then seeking possession, the role of Poplar is so closely assimilated to that of Tower Hamlets that it was performing public and not private functions. Poplar therefore is a functional public authority, at least to that extent. We emphasise that this does not mean that all Poplar's functions are public. We do not even decide that the position would be the same if the defendant was a secure tenant. The activities of housing associations can be ambiguous. For example, their activities in raising private or public finance could be very different from those that are under consideration here. The raising of finance by Poplar could well be a private function.*

The reasoning here has been criticised. Craig has argued that 'rights-based protections should not depend on the method of service delivery. ... It is difficult to see why the nature of a function should alter if it is contracted out, rather than being performed in house. If it is a public function when undertaken in house, it should be equally so when contracted out' (Craig, 2002). Davies has suggested that 'any gap in the availability of duties or remedies is particularly concerning because it gives rise to inequality in the treatment of different claimants depending on the arrangements a public authority has made for service delivery' (Davies, 2008, p. 233). In circumstances where wider public policy goals are included as outcomes in public contracts, perhaps the performance of those contracts is less of a private matter between the contracting authority and the contractor. In the UK, this will likely be very fact-specific in any individual case – despite any wider constitutional concerns.

5.3 Inherently governmental

In 2018, UK construction and services giant Carillion collapsed under £1.3 billion of debt (Mor, 2018). At the time of its collapse, Carillion was contracted to deliver a wide range of services to the Ministry of Defence, the Ministry of Justice, major public transportation systems, hospitals, local councils, and schools. In the aftermath of its collapse, the House of Commons Public Administration and Constitutional Affairs Committee asked three key questions (2018): (i) how appropriate is it for particular public sector projects or services to be run by the private sector?; (ii) is the government just the customer or does it have wider responsibilities as the steward of these markets?; and (iii) what capability does the government still lack in letting and managing contracts?

The Committee report did not arrive at a clear answer to on what should remain within government and what should be contracted for:

> *At different times, private, charitable, and public providers have both succeeded and failed to contribute to successful public services. All the witnesses to our inquiry accepted that the public sector should buy in some goods or services from the private sector, and should insist on providing others internally.* **The public sector should not contract out the final decision making about policy. The public sector always retains responsibility for the entitlement of individuals to benefits or services.** *Whether ordinary services should be outsourced though will depend upon the capacity of the public sector, private sector or voluntary sector to deliver them, the comparative cost, and ultimately, the value that each provider can produce.* (House of Commons, 2018, p 11, emphasis added)

However, the Committee was very conscious of the government's role as superior holder of risk and was very concerned about whether contractors should take on risks that should remain with the government. The Committee was especially concerned about contract models that tie payment to outcomes:

> *UK governments have often transferred risks to contractors that they cannot possibly manage. This is driven, in part, by the decision to use contractual models such as payment by results which involve risk transnfer on a huge scale. The transfer of large amounts of risk is often counter-productive: leading to more conservative approaches to service delivery. This situation has been made worse by the fact that governments have often not understood fully the services or projects they have wanted the private sector to manage and without any understanding or data about the assets being handed over.* (House of Commons, 2018, p. 23)

The US federal government is prohibited from using contracts to perform 'inherently government functions', which it defines as 'a function that is so intimately related to the public interest as to mandate performance by government employees' (FAR 7.5). The FAR goes on to underscore that 'this definition is a policy determination, not a legal determination', whereby inherently governmental functions include 'the exercise of discretion in applying Government authority' or the 'act of governing', and 'the making of value judgements in making decisions for the Government' as in monetary transactions and entitlements (FAR Part 2).

A 2011 White House policy letter highlights the management and capacity issues related to inherently governmental functions, requiring agencies to 'take special care to retain sufficient management oversight over how contractors are used to support government operations and ensure that Federal employees have the technical skills and expertise needed to maintain control of the agency mission and operations' (OMB, 2011). The same policy letter also highlights management and capacity issues related to contact performance of functions that are closely related to inherently governmental functions, are critical functions, or 'where, due to the nature of the contract services provided, there is a potential for confusion as to whether work is being performed by government employees or contractors' (OMB, 2011). In these circumstances, the policy letter states: 'Contract management should be appropriate to the nature of the contract, ensure that government officials are performing oversight at all times, and make clear to other government organizations or to the public when citizens are receiving service from contractors' (OMB, 2011).

We maintain that identifying what is inherently governmental or deciding where to retain democratically legitimated decision-making procedures, accountability mechanisms, and safeguards is not straightforward, especially when contracting for outcomes. As we have detailed throughout this Element, the emphasis of applied public administration and public policy scholarship tends to be on estimating the efficiency and performance of contracting out. A problem with these kinds of analyses is that in any individual scenario before a public manager, the procedures, accountability mechanisms, and safeguards we value in a democratic society look like costs. Such economic arguments are limited in that they conceive of public good as an aggregation of private interest (Mazzucato, 2023) rather than recognising the unique ability the state to deliver public value. Hence, the benefits of oversight functions are best viewed with an orientation that understands that the continued legitimacy of civil servants and government action is inexplicably tied to their ability to account for decisions in policy design and implementation (Stone, 1983).

The law cannot provide us with a list of inherently governmental functions or lists of services where we want or do not want democratically informed decision-making procedures, accountability mechanisms, and safeguards. Likewise, managerial sciences and applied economics cannot fully calculate the costs and benefits of including such oversight and safeguards. Hence, the big challenge of linking policy designs to implementation via outcomes-based contracts is the risk that public managers set outcomes as a way of circumventing meaningful government presence during service delivery or assume that an illusory 'perfect contract' will make services self-implementing and outcomes automatically achievable.

References

Agranoff, R. (2003) *Leveraging Networks: A Guide for Public Managers Working across Organizations*. Washington DC: IBM Endowment for the Business of Government. www.businessofgovernment.org/sites/default/files/LeveragingNetworks.pdf (Accessed: 18 July 2023).

Agranoff, R. and McGuire, M. (2001) 'Big questions in public network management research', *Journal of Public Administration Research and Theory*, 11(3), pp. 295–326. https://doi.org/10.1093/oxfordjournals.jpart.a003504.

Alonso, J. M., Clifton, J. and Díaz-Fuentes, D. (2015) 'Did new public management matter? An empirical analysis of the outsourcing and decentralization effects on public sector size', *Public Management Review*, 17(5), pp. 643–660. https://doi.org/10.1080/14719037.2013.822532.

Anders, J. and Dorsett, R. (2017) *Peterborough Social Impact Bond: Final Report on Cohort 2 Analysis*. London: Ministry of Justice. www.gov.uk/government/publications/final-results-for-cohort-2-of-the-social-impact-bond-payment-by-results-pilot-at-hmp-peterborough (Accessed: 26 October 2022).

Ansell, C. and Torfing, J. (2016) *Handbook on Theories of Governance*. Cheltenham: Edward Elgar.

Ansell, C. and Gash, A. (2008) 'Collaborative Governance in Theory and Practice', *Journal of Public Administration Research and Theory*, 18(4), pp. 543–571. https://doi.org/10.1093/jopart/mum032.

Arrowsmith, S. (2010) 'Horizontal policies in public procurement: a taxonomy', *Journal of Public Procurement*, 10(2), pp. 149–186. https://doi.org/10.1108/JOPP-10-02-2010-B001.

Arrowsmith, S. and Trybus, M. (2002) *Public Procurement: The Continuing Revolution [electronic resource]*. Zuidpoolsingel: Wolters Kluwer Law & Business (Ebook central). https://ezproxy-prd.bodleian.ox.ac.uk/login?url=https://ebookcentral.proquest.com/lib/oxford/detail.action?docID=5088434 (Accessed: 31 July 2023).

Aucoin, P. (1990) 'Administrative reform in public management: Paradigms, principles, paradoxes and pendulums', *Governance*, 3(2), pp. 115–137. https://doi.org/10.1111/j.1468-0491.1990.tb00111.x.

Baker, K. and Stoker, G. (2012) 'Metagovernance and nuclear power in Europe', *Journal of European Public Policy*, 19(7), pp. 1026–1051. https://doi.org/10.1080/13501763.2011.652900.

References

Baker, K. and Stoker, G. (2013) 'Governance and Nuclear Power: Why Governing is Easier Said than Done', *Political Studies*, 61(3), pp. 580–598. https://doi.org/10.1111/j.1467-9248.2012.00978.x

Baltrunaite, A., Giorgiantonio, C., Mocetti, S., Orlando, Tommaso. (2021) 'Discretion and supplier selection in public procurement', *Journal of Law, Economics, & Organization*, 37(1), pp. 134–167. https://doi.org/10.1093/jleo/ewaa009.

Barnow, B. S. (2000) 'Exploring the relationship between performance management and program impact: A case study of the job training partnership act', *Journal of Policy Analysis and Management*, 19(1), pp. 118–141. https://doi.org/10.1002/(SICI)1520-6688(200024)19:1<118::AID-PAM7>3.0.CO;2-4.

Berry, F. S. (1994) 'Innovation in Public Management: The Adoption of Strategic Planning', *Public Administration Review*, 54(4), pp. 322–330. https://doi.org/10.2307/977379.

Bezdek, B. L. (2000) 'Contractual welfare: Non-accountability and diminished democracy in local government contracts for welfare-to-work services tenth anual symposium on contemporary urban challenges – Redefining the public sector: Accountability and democracy in the era of privatization', *Fordham Urban Law Journal*, 28(5), pp. 1559–1610.

Boston, J. (2011) 'Basic NPM ideas and their development', in Christensen T. and Lægreid P. (eds) *The Ashgate Research Companion to New Public Management*. London: Routledge, pp. 17–32.

Bovaird, T. and Davies, R. (2011) 'Chapter 7 outcome-based service commissioning and delivery: Does it make a difference?', in *Research in Public Policy Analysis and Management*. Leeds Emerald, pp. 93–114.

Brown, T. L., Potoski, M. and Van Slyke, D. M. (2006) 'Managing public service contracts: Aligning values, institutions, and markets', *Public Administration Review*, 66(3), pp. 323–331.

Brown, T. L., Potoski, M. and Van Slyke, D. M. (2018) 'Complex contracting: Management challenges and solutions', *Public Administration Review*, 78(5), pp. 739–747. https://doi.org/10.1111/puar.12959.

Bryson, J. M., Crosby, B. C. and Bloomberg, L. (2014) 'Public value governance: Moving beyond traditional public administration and the new public management', *Public Administration Review*, 74(4), pp. 445–456. https://doi.org/10.1111/puar.12238.

Carter, E., FitzGerald, C., Dixon, R., et al. (2018) *Building the Tools for Public Services to Secure*. Oxford: University of Oxford, p. 21. https://waystowellness.org.uk/site/assets/files/1317/2018-bsg-golab-evidencereport.pdf.

Carter, E. (2020) 'Debate: Would a social impact bond by any other name smell as sweet? Stretching the model and why it might matter', *Public Money &*

Management, 40(3), pp. 183–185. https://doi.org/10.1080/09540962.2020.1714288.

Carter, E. (2021) 'More than marketised? Exploring the governance and accountability mechanisms at play in Social Impact Bonds', *Journal of Economic Policy Reform*, 24(1), pp. 78–94. https://doi.org/10.1080/17487870.2019.1575736.

Carter, E. and Ball, N. (2021) 'Spotlighting shared outcomes for social impact programs that work (SSIR)', *Stanford Social Innovation Review*. https://doi.org/10.48558/84ZM-1Z65 (Accessed: 14 June 2023).

Carter, E., Rosenbach, F., Domingos, F., & van Lier, F. A. (2024). Contracting 'person-centred' working by results: street-level managers and frontline experiences in an outcomes-based contract. *Public Management Review*, 1–19. https://doi.org/10.1080/14719037.2024.2342398.

Carter, E. and Whitworth, A. (2015) 'Creaming and parking in quasi-marketised welfare-to-work schemes: Designed out of or designed In to the UK work programme?', *Journal of Social Policy*, 44(2), pp. 277–296. https://doi.org/10.1017/S0047279414000841.

Cashore, B. and Howlett, M. (2007) 'Punctuating which equilibrium? Understanding thermostatic policy dynamics in Pacific Northwest Forestry', *American Journal of Political Science*, 51(3), pp. 532–551. https://doi.org/10.1111/j.1540-5907.2007.00266.x.

Christens, B. D. and Inzeo, P. T. (2015) 'Widening the view: Situating collective impact among frameworks for community-led change', *Community Development*, 46(4), pp. 420–435. https://doi.org/10.1080/15575330.2015.1061680.

Christensen, R. K., Goerdel, H. T. and Nicholson-Crotty, S. (2011) 'Management, law, and the pursuit of the public good in public administration', *Journal of Public Administration Research and Theory*, 21(suppl_1), pp. i125–i140. https://doi.org/10.1093/jopart/muq065.

Cibinic, J., Nash, R. C., and George Washington University Government Contracts Program (1998) *Formation of Government Contracts*. 3rd ed. George Washington University Law School, Government Contracts Program, Washington DC.

Coase, R. H. (1937) 'The nature of the firm', *Economica*, 4(16), pp. 386–405.

Coviello, D., Guglielmo, A. and Spagnolo, G. (2017) 'The Effect of Discretion on Procurement Performance | Management Science', *Management Science*, 64(2), pp. 715–738. https://doi.org/10.1287/mnsc.2016.2628.

Crozier, M., Huntington, S. P., and Watanuki, J. (1975) *Crisis of Democracy: Report on the Governability of Democracies to the Trilateral Commission*. New York: New York University Press.

Craig, P. (2002) 'Contracting out, the Human Rights Act and the scope of judicial review', *Law Quarterly Review*, 118, pp. 551–568.

Dadush, S. (2022) 'Prosocial contracts: Making relational contracts more relational contract in crises', *Law and Contemporary Problems*, 85(2), pp. 153–175.

Dragos, D. C., Halonen, K. and Treumer, S. (eds) (2023) *Contract Changes: The Dark Side of EU Procurement Law*. Cheltenham, UK: Edward Elgar Publishing Ltd.

Davies, A. C. L. (2008) *The Public Law of Government Contracts*. Oxford University Press. Oxford, UK.

Davies, A. C. L., Buys, E. and Macdonald, J. R. (2023) 'Accountability for "social value" in procurement', *Public Law*, (April), pp. 214–223.

Dayson, C., Fraser, A. and Lowe, T. (2020) 'A comparative analysis of social impact bond and conventional financing approaches to health service commissioning in England: The case of social prescribing', *Journal of Comparative Policy Analysis: Research and Practice*, 22(2), pp. 153–169. https://doi.org/10.1080/13876988.2019.1643614.

De Pieri, B., Chiodo, V. and Gerli, F. (2022) 'Based on outcomes? Challenges and (missed) opportunities of measuring social outcomes in outcome-based contracting', *International Public Management Journal*, 26(3), pp. 1–26. Available at: https://doi.org/10.1080/10967494.2022.2077490.

Diller, M. (2001) 'Form and substance in the privatization of poverty programs symposium: New forms of governance: Ceding public power to private actors', *UCLA Law Review*, 49(6), pp. 1739–1766.

Dimand, A.-M. and Cheng, S. (2023) 'Bottom-up innovation adoption of green public procurement in the United States', *Local Government Studies*, 49(6), pp. 1359–1385. https://doi.org/10.1080/03003930.2022.2161523.

Disley, E., Giacomantonio, C., Kruithof, K., Sim, M. (2016) *The payment by results Social Impact Bond pilot at HMP Peterborough: Final process evaluation report*. RAND Corporation. www.rand.org/pubs/research_reports/RR1212.html (Accessed: 30 June 2022).

Domberger, S. and Jensen, P. (1997) 'Contracting out by the public sector: Theory, evidence, prospects', *Oxford Review of Economic Policy*, 13(4), pp. 67–78. https://doi.org/10.1093/oxrep/13.4.67.

DWP (2012) 'Innovation Fund Key facts'. UK Department for Work and Pensions. https://assets.publishing.service.gov.uk/government/uploads/system/uploads/attachment_data/file/212328/hmg_g8_factsheet.pdf (Accessed: 31 July 2023).

Elsby. A., Smith, T. R., Monk, L., and Ronicle, J. (2022) *Using impact bonds in education in low- and middle-income countries: An evidence review*. 170411.

Washington DC: World Bank. https://documents.worldbank.org/en/publication/documents-reports/documentdetail/099846504132230407/idu02b848900027dd04d480a179090d86b2071a4 (Accessed: 31 July 2023).

Economy, C., Carter, E. and Airoldi, M. (2022) 'Have we "stretched" social impact bonds too far? An empirical analysis of SIB design in practice', *International Public Management Journal*, 26(3), pp. 413–436. https://doi.org/10.1080/10967494.2022.2077867.

Emerson, K. and Nabatchi, T. (2015) *Collaborative Governance Regimes*. Washington DC: Georgetown University Press.

European Commission (2016) *Stock-taking of administrative capacity, systems and practices across the EU to ensure the compliance and quality of public procurement involving European Structural and Investment (ESI) Funds*. European Commission. https://data.europa.eu/doi/10.2776/311087.

European Commission (2017) *Building an architecture for the professionalisation of public procurement: library of good practices and tools*. Website. https://op.europa.eu:443/en/publication-detail/-/publication/5fe2a634-bd85-11e9-9d01-01aa75ed71a1/language-en (Accessed: 17 November 2019).

European Commission (2020) *ProcurCompEU - European Competency Framework for Public Procurement Professionals*. Luxembourg: Publications Office of the European Union.

European Commission (2021) *Buying Social. A Guide to Taking Account of Social Considerations in Public Procurement*. European Commission.

Ferlie, E., Ashburner, L., Fitzgerald, L., Pettigrew, A. (1996) *The New Public Management in Action*. Oxford: Oxford University Press. https://doi.org/10.1093/acprof:oso/9780198289029.001.0001.

Ferlie, E. (2017) *The New Public Management and Public Management Studies, Oxford Research Encyclopedia of Business and Management*. Oxford: Oxford University Press. https://doi.org/10.1093/acrefore/9780190224851.013.129.

FitzGerald, C., Carter, E., Dixon, R., Airoldi, M. (2019) 'Walking the contractual tightrope: A transaction cost economics perspective on social impact bonds', *Public Money & Management*, 39(7), pp. 458–467. https://doi.org/10.1080/09540962.2019.1583889.

FitzGerald, C., Hameed, T., Rosenbach, F., et al. (2021) *Life Chances Fund Introductory Primary Evaluation Report*. www.gov.uk/government/publications/life-chances-fund-introductory-primary-evaluation-report (Accessed: 16 February 2022).

FitzGerald, C., Rosenbach, F., Hameed, T., et al. (2021) 'New development: Rallying together—The rationale for and structure of collaborative practice in England', *Public Money & Management*, 42(5), pp. 349–352. https://doi.org/10.1080/09540962.2021.1981628.

FitzGerald, C., Tan, S., Carter, E., Airoldi, M. (2023) 'Contractual acrobatics: A configurational analysis of outcome specifications and payment in outcome-based contracts', *Public Management Review*, 25(9), pp. 1796–1814. https://doi.org/10.1080/14719037.2023.2244501.

FitzGerald, C., Fraser, A., Kimmitt, J., Knoll, L. and Williams, J. (2023) 'Outcomes-based contracting and public management reform: Lessons from a decade of experimentation', *International Public Management Journal*, 26(3), pp. 329–338. https://doi.org/10.1080/10967494.2023.2170504.

FitzGerald, C., Fraser, A. and Kimmitt, J. (2020) 'Tackling the big questions in social impact bond research through comparative approaches', *Journal of Comparative Policy Analysis: Research and Practice*, 22(2), pp. 85–99. https://doi.org/10.1080/13876988.2020.1726177.

Fraser, A., Tan, S., Lagarde, M., Mays, N. (2018) 'Narratives of promise, narratives of caution: A review of the literature on social impact bonds', *Social Policy & Administration*, 52(1), pp. 4–28. https://doi.org/10.1111/spol.12260.

Fraser, A., Knoll, L. and Hevenstone, D. (2022) 'Contested social impact bonds: Welfare conventions, conflicts and compromises in five European active-labor market programs', *International Public Management Journal*, 26(3), pp. 339–356. https://doi.org/10.1080/10967494.2022.2089792.

Freeman, J. (2000) 'The private role in public governance', *NYU Law Review*, 75. www.nyulawreview.org/issues/volume-75-number-3/the-private-role-in-public-governance/ (Accessed: 14 January 2024).

French, M., Kimmitt, J., Wilson, R., Jamieson, D., Lowe, T. (2022) 'Social impact bonds and public service reform: Back to the future of New Public Management?', *International Public Management Journal*, 26(3), pp. 376–395. https://doi.org/10.1080/10967494.2022.2050859.

Frydlinger, D., Hart, O. and Vitasek, K. (2019) 'A New Approach to Contracts', *Harvard Business Review*, 1 September. https://hbr.org/2019/09/a-new-approach-to-contracts (Accessed: 30 December 2023).

Gibson, M. (2023) 'Debate: In contracts, we trust—managing risk in public contracts through a relational approach', *Public Money & Management*, 43(2), pp. 83–84. https://doi.org/10.1080/09540962.2022.2133767.

Gilson, R. J., Sabel, C. F. and Scott, R. E. (2010) Braiding: The interaction of formal and informal contracting in theory, practice and doctrine. Stanford Law and Economics Olin Working Paper No. 389, Columbia Law and Economics Working Paper No. 367. https://doi.org/10.2139/ssrn.1535575.

Golka, P. (2022). The allure of finance: Social impact investing and the challenges of assetization in financialized capitalism. *Economy and Society*, 52(1), 62–86. https://doi.org/10.1080/03085147.2023.2151221.

Government Outcomes Lab (2019) *Outcomes-based contracting*. https://golab.bsg.ox.ac.uk/the-basics/outcomes-based-contracting/

Grand, J. L. (1991) 'The theory of government failure', *British Journal of Political Science*, 21(4), pp. 423–442. https://doi.org/10.1017/S0007123400006244.

Griffiths, R., Thomas, A. and Pemberton, A. (2016) *Qualitative evaluation of the DWP Innovation Fund: Final Report*. https://assets.publishing.service.gov.uk/government/uploads/system/uploads/attachment_data/file/535032/rr922-qualitative-evaluation-of-the-dwp-innovation-fund-final-report.pdf (Accessed: 30 June 2022).

Gueorguieva, V., Accius, J., Apaza, C., Bennet, L., Brownley, C., Cronin, S. et al. (2009) 'The Program Assessment Rating Tool and the Government Performance and Results Act: Evaluating Conflicts and Disconnections', *The American Review of Public Administration*, 39(3), pp. 225–245. https://doi.org/10.1177/0275074008319218.

Gulati, R., John, T., & Köhler, B. (2023). The Elgar Companion to UNCITRAL (1st ed.). Edward Elgar Publishing Limited. https://doi.org/10.4337/9781803924540.

Gustafsson-Wright, E., Gardiner, S. and Putcha, V. (2015) *The Potential and Limitations of Impact Bonds*. Washington DC : Brookings Institute. https://golab.bsg.ox.ac.uk/knowledge-bank/resources/potential-and-limitations-impact-bonds/ (Accessed: 31 March 2023).

Hajer, J. (2020) 'The National Governance and Policy Context of Social Impact Bond Emergence: A Comparative Analysis of Leaders and Skeptics', *Journal of Comparative Policy Analysis: Research and Practice*, 22(2), pp. 116–133. https://doi.org/10.1080/13876988.2019.1695924.

Hajer, J. and Loxley, J. (2021) *Social Service, Private Gain: The Political Economy of Social Impact Bonds*. Toronto: University of Toronto Press.

Hale, T. (2016) '"All hands on deck": The Paris agreement and nonstate climate action', *Global Environmental Politics*, 16(3), pp. 12–22. https://doi.org/10.1162/GLEP_a_00362.

Halligan, J. (2011) 'NPM in anglo-saxon countries', in T. Christensen and P. Lægreid (eds) *The Ashgate Research Companion to New Public Management*. London: Routledge, pp. 83–96.

Hansen, H. F. (2011) 'NPM in scandinavia', in T. Christensen and P. Lægreid (eds) *The Ashgate Research Companion to New Public Management*. London: Routledge, pp. 113–130.

Hart, O. D. (1988) 'Incomplete contracts and the theory of the firm conference papers to celebrate the fiftieth anniversary of the nature of the firm', *Journal of Law, Economics & Organization*, 4(1), pp. 119–140.

Heckman, J. J., Heinrich, C. J., Courty, P., Marschke, G., Smith, J. A. (eds) (2011) *The Performance of Performance Standards*. Kalamazoo, Mich: W. E. Upjohn Institute for Employment Research. https://doi.org/10.17848/9780880993982.

Hefetz, A. and Warner, M. (2004) 'Privatization and Its Reverse: Explaining the Dynamics of the Government Contracting Process', *Journal of Public Administration Research and Theory: J-PART*, 14(2), pp. 171–190.

Heinrich, C. J. and Kabourek, S. E. (2019) 'Pay-for-success development in the United States: Feasible or failing to launch?', *Public Administration Review*, 79(6), pp. 867–879. https://doi.org/10.1111/puar.13099.

Heinrich, C. J. and Marschke, G. (2010) 'Incentives and their dynamics in public sector performance management systems', *Journal of Policy Analysis and Management*, 29(1), pp. 183–208. https://doi.org/10.1002/pam.20484.

Hevenstone, D., Fraser, A., Hobi, L., Przepiorka, W., Geuke, G. G. M. (2023) 'The impact of social impact bond financing', *Public Administration* Review, 83(4), pp. 930–946 [Preprint]. https://kclpure.kcl.ac.uk/portal/en/publications/the-impact-of-social-impact-bond-financing(9b8be82f-73f2-4a5f-b0fe-e8cee91a36a2).html (Accessed: 31 March 2023).

Hood, C. (1991) 'A public management for all seasons?', *Public Administration*, 69(1), pp. 3–19. https://doi.org/10.1111/j.1467-9299.1991.tb00779.x.

Hood, C. (1986) *The Tools of Government*. Chatham House Publishers.

Hood, C. (1995) 'Emerging Issues in Public Administration', *Public Administration*, 73(1), pp. 165–183. https://doi.org/10.1111/j.1467-9299.1995.tb00822.x.

Hood, C. C. and Margetts, H. Z. (2007) *The Tools of Government in the Digital Age: 10*. 2nd ed. Basingstoke: Palgrave.

Hood, C. and Dixon, R. (2015) *A Government that Worked Better and Cost Less?: Evaluating Three Decades of Reform and Change in UK Central Government*. Oxford: Oxford University Press.

Hood, C. and Dixon, R. (2016) 'Not what it said on the tin? Reflections on three decades of UK public management reform', *Financial Accountability & Management*, 32(4), pp. 409–428. https://doi.org/10.1111/faam.12095.

Hood, C. and Peters, G. (2004) 'The middle aging of new public management: Into the age of paradox?', *Journal of Public Administration Research and Theory*, 14(3), pp. 267–282. https://doi.org/10.1093/jopart/muh019.

House of Commons Public Administration and Constitutional Affairs Committee (2018) *After Carillion: Public sector outsourcing and contracting*. HC 748. House of Commons, p. 55.

Howlett, M., Ramesh, M. and Capano, G. (2022) 'The role of tool calibrations and policy specifications in policy change: evidence from healthcare reform efforts in Korea 1990-2020', *Journal of Asian Public Policy*, 17(1), pp. 1–20. https://doi.org/10.1080/17516234.2022.2030276.

Howlett, M.P., Ramesh, M. and Capano, G. (2023) 'The Micro-Dimensions of Policy Design: A Key Challenge for Real-World Policy Practice'. Rochester. https://doi.org/10.2139/ssrn.4410177.

Hunt, F. (2020) '$13 Trillion – The Global Value Of Public Procurement', *Spend Network*. https://spendnetwork.com/blog/13-trillion-the-global-value-of-public-procurement (Accessed: 31 July 2023).

ICF (2019) *Fair Chance Fund Evaluation: Final Report*. www.gov.uk/government/publications/fair-chance-fund-evaluation-final-report (Accessed: 18 January 2024).

INDIGO (2023) *Impact Bond Dataset*. https://golab.bsg.ox.ac.uk/knowledge-bank/indigo/impact-bond-dataset-v2/ (Accessed: 31 March 2023).

Janssen, W. and Caranta, R. (2023) *Mandatory Sustainability Requirements in EU Public Procurement Law: Reflections on a Paradigm Shift*. London: Hart.

Johnston, J. M. and Romzek, B. S. (2008) 'Social Welfare Contracts as Networks', *Administration & Society*, 40(2), pp. 115–146. https://doi.org/10.1177/0095399707312826.

Kelman, S. (1990) *Procurement and Public Management: The Fear of Discretion and the Quality of Government Performance*. Washington, D.C.: American Enterprise Institute.

Kirkpatrick, I. and Lucio, M. M. (1996) 'Introduction: the contract state and the future of public management', *Public Administration*, 74(1), pp. 1–8. https://doi.org/10.1111/j.1467-9299.1996.tb00854.x.

Kohli, J., Besharov, D. and Costa, K. (2012) *What Are Social Impact Bonds?* www.americanprogress.org/article/what-are-social-impact-bonds/ (Accessed: 1 May 2024).

Koliba, C., Mills, R. and Zia, A. (2011) 'Accountability in Governance Networks: An Assessment of Public, Private, and Nonprofit Emergency Management Practices Following Hurricane Katrina', *Public Administration Review*, 71(2), pp. 210–220. https://doi.org/10.1111/j.1540-6210.2011.02332.x.

Koliba, C. J., Meek, J. W., Zia, A., Mills, R. W. (2019) *Governance Networks in Public Administration and Public Policy*. New York: Routledge.

Lake, R. W. (2015) 'The financialization of urban policy in the age of Obama', *Journal of Urban Affairs*, 37(1), pp. 75–78. https://doi.org/10.1111/juaf.12167.

Lazzarini, S. (2020) 'The nature of the social firm: Alternative organizational forms for social value creation and appropriation', *Academy of Management Review*, 45(3), pp. 620–645.

Lazzarini, S. G. (2022) *The Right Privatization: Why Private Firms in Public Initiatives Need Capable Governments*. Cambridge: Cambridge University Press.

Liebman, J. and Sellman, A. (2013) *Social Impact Bonds A Guide for State and Local Governments*. Harvard Kennedy School Social Impact Bond Technical Assistance Lab. https://hkssiblab.wordpress.com/wp-content/uploads/2013/07/social-impact-bonds-a-guide-for-state-and-local-governments.pdf (Accessed: 1 May 2024).

Macaulay, S. (1963) 'Non-contractual relations in business: A preliminary study', *American Sociological Review*, 28(1), pp. 55–67. https://doi.org/10.2307/2090458.

Macneil, I. R. (1973) 'The many futures of contracts', *Southern California Law Review*, 47, p. 691.

Macneil, I. R. (1977) 'Contracts: Adjustment of long-term economic relations under classical, neoclassical, and relational contract law', *Northwestern University Law Review*, 72(6), pp. 854–905.

Makgill, I., Yeung, A. and Marchessault, L. (2020) *How Governments Spend: Opening Up the Value of Global Public Procurement*. Open Contracting Partnership & Spend Network. www.open-contracting.org/wp-content/uploads/2020/08/OCP2020-Global-Public-Procurement-Spend.pdf.

Mandell, M. and Steelman, T. (2003) 'Understanding what can be accomplished through interorganizational innovations The importance of typologies, context and management strategies', *Public Management Review*, 5(2), pp. 197–224. https://doi.org/10.1080/1461667032000066417.

Mazzucato, M. (2023) 'Governing the economics of the common good: from correcting market failures to shaping collective goals', *Journal of Economic Policy Reform*, 27(1), pp. 1–24.

McCrudden, C. (2007) *Buying Social Justice: Equality, Government Procurement, and Legal Change*. Oxford; Oxford University Press.

McGuire, M. (2006) 'Collaborative public management: Assessing what we know and how we know it', *Public Administration Review*, 66(s1), pp. 33–43. https://doi.org/10.1111/j.1540-6210.2006.00664.x.

Milward, H. B. (1996) 'Symposium on the Hollow State: Capacity, Control, and Performance in Interorganizational Settings', *Journal of Public Administration Research and Theory*, 6(2), pp. 193–196. https://doi.org/10.1093/oxfordjournals.jpart.a024306.

Milward, H. B. and Provan, K. G. (2000) 'Governing the hollow state', *Journal of Public Administration Research and Theory: J-PART*, 10(2), pp. 359–379.

Molin, M. D. and Masella, C. (2016) 'Networks in policy, management and governance: A comparative literature review to stimulate future research avenues', *Journal of Management & Governance*, 20(4), pp. 823–849. https://doi.org/10.1007/s10997-015-9329-x.

Mor, F. (2018) 'Carillion collapse: what went wrong?' https://commonslibrary.parliament.uk/carillion-collapse-what-went-wrong/ (Accessed: 18 January 2024).

Moynihan, D. P., Fernandez, S., Kim, S., LeRoux, K., Piotrowski, S. K., Wright, B. E. et al. (2011) 'Performance Regimes Amidst Governance Complexity', *Journal of Public Administration Research and Theory*, 21(suppl 1), pp. i141–i155. https://doi.org/10.1093/jopart/muq059.

Moynihan, D. P. and Kroll, A. (2016) 'Performance Management Routines That Work? An Early Assessment of the GPRA Modernization Act', *Public Administration Review*, 76(2), pp. 314–323. https://doi.org/10.1111/puar.12434.

Mulgan, G., Reeder, N., Aylott, M., Bo'sher, L. (2011) 'Social impact investment: The challenge and opportunity of social impact Bonds', p. 38. https://youngfoundation.org/wp-content/uploads/2012/10/Social-Impact-Investment-The-opportunity-and-challenge-of-Social-Impact-Bonds-March-2011.pdf.

Nagle, J. (1999) *A History of Government Contracting*. 2nd ed. https://scholarship.law.gwu.edu/history_gov_contracting/2.

Nagle, J. (2012) *A History of Government Contracting*. 3rd ed. Government Training Inc. https://scholarship.law.gwu.edu/history_gov_contracting/4.

Newhouse, J. P. (1984) 'Cream skimming, asymmetric information, and a competitive insurance market', *Journal of Health Economics*, 3(1), pp. 97–100. https://doi.org/10.1016/0167-6296(84)90030-4.

Niskanen, W. A. (2017) *Bureaucracy & Representative Government*. New York: Routledge. https://doi.org/10.4324/9781315081878.

OECD (2021) *Government at a Glance 2021*. Paris: Organisation for Economic Co-operation and Development. https://doi.org/10.1787/1c258f55-en (Accessed: 6 January 2024).

OECD (2023) *Professionalising the Public Procurement Workforce: A Review of Current Initiatives and Challenges*. Policy Paper 26. Paris: OECD Publishing. www.oecd.org/publications/professionalising-the-public-procurement-workforce-e2eda150-en.htm.

Olson, H., Painter, G., Albertson, K. Fox, C. and O'Leary, C. et al. (2024) 'Are Social Impact Bonds an Innovation in Finance or Do They Help Finance Social Innovation?', *Journal of Social Policy*, 53(2), pp. 407–431. doi:10.1017/S0047279422000356.

O'Leary, R. and Vij, N. (2012) 'Collaborative public management: Where have we been and where are we going?', *The American Review of Public Administration*, 42(5), pp. 507–522. https://doi.org/10.1177/0275074012445780.

OMB (2011) 'Publication of the Office of Federal Procurement Policy (OFPP) Policy Letter 11–01, Performance of Inherently Governmental and Critical Functions'. www.federalregister.gov/documents/2011/09/12/2011-23165/publication-of-the-office-of-federal-procurement-policy-ofpp-policy-letter-11-01-performance-of (Accessed: 6 March 2022).

Osborne, S. P. (2006) 'The new public governance?', *Public Management Review*, 8(3), pp. 377–387. https://doi.org/10.1080/14719030600853022.

Osborne, S. P. (ed.) (2010) *The New Public Governance? Emerging Perspectives on the Theory and Practice of Public Governance*. London: Routledge.

Ostrom, E. (2010) 'Beyond markets and states: Polycentric governance of complex economic systems', *American Economic Review*, 100(3), pp. 641–672. https://doi.org/10.1257/aer.100.3.641.

Peters, B. G., Capano, G., Howlett, M., et al. (2018) 'Designing for Policy Effectiveness: Defining and Understanding a Concept', *Elements in Public Policy* [Preprint]. https://doi.org/10.1017/9781108555081.

Petersen, O. H., Hjelmar, U. and Vrangbæk, K. (2018) 'Is contracting out of public services still the great Panacea? A systematic review of studies on economic and quality effects from 2000 to 2014', *Social Policy & Administration*, 52(1), pp. 130–157. https://doi.org/10.1111/spol.12297.

Petersen, O. H., Houlberg, K. and Christensen, L. R. (2015) 'Contracting out local services: A tale of technical and social services', *Public Administration Review*, 75(4), pp. 560–570. https://doi.org/10.1111/puar.12367.

Pollitt, C. (2009) 'Bureaucracies remember, post-bureaucratic organizations forget?', *Public Administration*, 87(2), pp. 198–218. https://doi.org/10.1111/j.1467-9299.2008.01738.x.

Pollitt, C. and Bouckaert, G. (2017) *Public Management Reform: A Comparative Analysis – Into The Age of Austerity*. 4th ed. Oxford, New York: Oxford University Press.

Pollitt, C. (1990) *Managerialism and the Public Services: The Anglo-American Experience*. Basil Blackwell.

Provan, K. G. and Kenis, P. (2008) 'Modes of network governance: Structure, management, and effectiveness', *Journal of Public Administration Research and Theory*, 18(2), pp. 229–252. https://doi.org/10.1093/jopart/mum015.

Roberts, T. (2013) 'The Centre for Social Impact Bonds – Civil Service Quarterly'. https://quarterly.blog.gov.uk/2013/10/22/the-centre-for-social-impact-bonds/ (Accessed: 30 June 2022).

Roman, J. (2015) *Solving the Wrong Pockets Problem: How Pay for Success Promotes Investment in Evidence-Based Best Practices*. Washington, DC: Urban Institute. https://www.urban.org/sites/default/files/alfresco/publication-pdfs/2000427-Solving-the-Wrong-Pockets-Problem.pdf.

Ronicle, J. and Smith, K. (2020) *Youth Engagement Fund Evaluation – Final Report*. www.gov.uk/government/publications/youth-engagement-fund-evaluation-final-report (Accessed: 11 April 2023).

Ronicle, J., Stanworth, N. and Wooldridge, R. (2022) *Commissioning Better Outcomes Evaluation 3rd Update Report*. Ecorys. https://golab.bsg.ox.ac.uk/knowledge-bank/resource-library/commissioning-better-outcomes-evaluation-3rd-update-report/.

Rosen, R. and Mays, N. (1998) 'The impact of the UK NHS purchaser–provider split on the `rational' introduction of new medical technologies', *Health Policy*, 43(2), pp. 103–123. https://doi.org/10.1016/S0168-8510(97)00091-2.

Rosenau, P. V. (2000) *Public-private Policy Partnerships*. Cambridge: MIT Press.

Rosenbloom, D. H., Kravchuk, R. S. and Clerkin, R. M. (2022) *Public Administration: Understanding Management, Politics, and Law in the Public Sector*. 9th ed. New York: Routledge. https://doi.org/10.4324/9781003198116.

Sainsbury, D. (2013) 'The Enabling State', *RSA Journal*, 159(5553), pp. 42–45.

Salamon, L.M. (1989) *Beyond Privatization: The Tools of Government Action*. Lanham, MD: Urban Institute Press.

Salamon, L. M. (2000) 'The New Governance and the Tools of Public Action: An Introduction Tenth Anual Symposium on Contemporary Urban Challenges – Redefining the Public Sector: Accountability and Democracy in the Era of Privatization', *Fordham Urban Law Journal*, 28(5), pp. 1611–1674.

Salis, S., Wishart, R. and McKay, S. (2018) *Evaluation of the Innovation Fund Pilot: Quantitative Assessment of Impact and Social Return on Investment*. 956. London: UK Department for Work & Pensions. https://assets.publishing.service.gov.uk/government/uploads/system/uploads/attachment_data/file/737021/evaluation-of-the-innovation-fund-pilot-quantitative-assessment-of-impact-and-social-return-on-investment.pdf.

Savas, E. S. (1987) *Privatization: The Key to Better Government*. Chatham, NJ: Chatham House Publishers.

Savell, L., Carter, E., Airoldi, M. (2022) *Understanding Outcomes Funds: A Guide for Practitioners, Governments and Donors*. https://golab.bsg.ox.ac.uk/knowledge-bank/resources/understanding-outcomes-funds-a-guide-for-practitioners-governments-and-donors/ (Accessed: 30 June 2022).

Schochet, P. Z., Burghardt, J. and McConnell, S. (2006) *National Job Corps Study and Longer-Term Follow-Up Study: Impact and Benefit-Cost Findings Using Survey and Summary Earnings Records Data*. Mathematica Policy Research Reports. Mathematica Policy Research. https://econpapers.repec.org/paper/mprmprres/8074f4e4499d4e2ab1de13747e00f14f.htm (Accessed: 17 April 2023).

References

Schooner, S. L. (2002) 'Desiderata: Objectives for a System of Government Contract Law', *SSRN Electronic Journal* [Preprint]. https://doi.org/10.2139/ssrn.304620.

Schooner, S.L. (2011) *Commercial Purchasing: The Chasm between the United States Government's Evolving Policy and Practice*. Rochester, NY. https://doi.org/10.2139/ssrn.285536.

Schooner, S. L. and Speidel, M. (2020) *'Warming Up' to Sustainable Procurement*. SSRN Scholarly Paper 3697429. Rochester, NY: Social Science Research Network. https://papers.ssrn.com/abstract=3697429 (Accessed: 24 April 2022).

Schooner, S. L. (2021) 'No time to waste: Embracing sustainable procurement to mitigate the accelerating climate crisis'. Rochester, NY. https://papers.ssrn.com/abstract=3980915 (Accessed: 2 October 2023).

Scott, R. E. (2000) 'The case for formalism in relational contract', *Northwestern University Law Review*, 94(3), pp. 847–876.

Section 809 Panel (2019) *A Roadmap to the Section 809 Panel Reports*. https://discover.dtic.mil/section-809-panel/.

Shiva, M., FitzGerald, C., Carter, E. and Airoldi, M. (2024). 'Beyond "make" or "buy": Evaluating value-for-money in public service delivery'. *Annals of Public and Cooperative Economics*. https://doi.org/10.1111/apce.12468.

Smith, M. and PracticalLawPublicSector (2022) *Decision-Making by Public Bodies: Avoiding Legal Challenge | Practical Law, Westlaw*. https://libguides.swansea.ac.uk/oscola/insight#:~:text=Westlaw%20Insight%20%26%20Practical%20Law%20Company&text=The%20reference%20should%20then%20include,numbers%20to%20pinpoint%20the%20reference.

Sørensen, E. and Torfing, J. (2009) 'Making governance networks effective and democratic through metagovernance', *Public Administration*, 87(2), pp. 234–258. https://doi.org/10.1111/j.1467-9299.2009.01753.x.

Stone, C. N. (1983) 'Whither the welfare state? professionalization, bureaucracy, and the market alternative', *Ethics*, 93(3), pp. 588–595. https://doi.org/10.1086/292470.

Swiss, J. E. (1992) 'Adapting Total Quality Management (TQM) to Government', *Public Administration Review*, 52(4), pp. 356–362. https://doi.org/10.2307/3110395.

Szucs, F. (2023) 'Discretion and Favoritism in Public Procurement', *Journal of the European Economic Association* [Preprint]. https://doi.org/10.1093/jeea/jvad017.

Thomas, A., Griffiths, D. R. and Pemberton, D. A. (2016) 'Qualitative evaluation of the DWP's Innovation Fund: Final report'. https://assets.publishing.service.gov.uk/media/5a819f76e5274a2e8ab54fc9/rr922-qualitative-evaluation-of-the-dwp-innovation-fund-final-report.pdf.

References

Torfing, J., Andersen, L. B., Greve, C., Klausen, K. K. (2020) 'Public Governance Paradigms: Competing and Co-Existing', in *Public Governance Paradigms*. Cheltenham: Edward Elgar. www.elgaronline.com/display/9781788971218/9781788971218.xml (Accessed: 30 May 2023).

Tse, A. E. and Warner, M. E. (2020a) 'A Policy Outcomes Comparison: Does SIB Market Discipline Narrow Social Rights?', *Journal of Comparative Policy Analysis: Research and Practice*, 22(2), pp. 134–152. https://doi.org/10.1080/13876988.2019.1609789.

Tse, A. E. and Warner, M. E. (2020b) 'The razor's edge: Social impact bonds and the financialization of early childhood services', *Journal of Urban Affairs*, 42(6), pp. 816–832. https://doi.org/10.1080/07352166.2018.1465347.

UK Cabinet Office (2011) *Growing the Social Investment Market: A vision and strategy*. Cabinet Office. https://assets.publishing.service.gov.uk/media/5a789e99ed915d07d35b11ab/404970_SocialInvestmentMarket_acc.pdf.

UK Cabinet Office (2020) 'Procurement Policy Note 06/20 – taking account of social value in the award of central government contracts'. www.gov.uk/government/publications/procurement-policy-note-0620-taking-account-of-social-value-in-the-award-of-central-government-contracts (Accessed: 31 July 2023).

UK Cabinet Office (2021) *Procurement Policy Note 05/21: National Procurement Policy Statement*. www.gov.uk/government/publications/procurement-policy-note-0521-national-procurement-policy-statement (Accessed: 30 May 2022).

UK Department for Digital Culture Media & Sport (DCMS) (2016) 'Life chances fund frequently asked questions'. https://assets.publishing.service.gov.uk/government/uploads/system/uploads/attachment_data/file/876934/LCF_FAQs_FINAL_DRAFT.pdf (Accessed: 30 June 2022).

UNCITRAL (2011) *UNCITRAL Model Law on Public Procurement (2011) | United Nations Commission On International Trade Law*. https://uncitral.un.org/en/texts/procurement/modellaw/public_procurement (Accessed 31 July 2023).

United States President's Blue Ribbon Commission on Defense Management (1986) A Quest for Excellence: Final Report to the President. District of Columbia: The Commission. https://hdl.handle.net/2027/mdp.39015014775566 (Accessed: 31 July 2023).

US Government (2022) Proposed Federal Acquisition Regulation rule: Disclosure of Greenhouse Gas Emissions and Climate-Related Financial Risk. www.federalregister.gov/documents/2022/12/23/2022-27884/federal-acquisition-regulation-disclosure-of-greenhouse-gas-emissions-and-climate-related-financial (Accessed: 18 December 2023).

US Office of Management and Budget (2021) Executive Order 13985 of January 20, 2021: Advancing Racial Equity and Support for Underserved

Communities Through the Federal Government. www.federalregister.gov/documents/2021/01/25/2021-01753/advancing-racial-equity-and-support-for-underserved-communities-through-the-federal-government (Accessed: 31 July 2023).

US Office of Management and Budget (2023) Memorandum for Chief Acquisition Officers Senior Procurement Executives: Federal Acquisition Certification in Contracting (FAC-C) Modernization. www.whitehouse.gov/wp-content/uploads/2023/01/FAC-C-Modernization-Memorandum-19-Jan-2023.pdf.

Van Slyke, D. M. (2003) 'The mythology of privatization in contracting for social services', *Public Administration Review*, 63(3), pp. 296–315. https://doi.org/10.1111/1540-6210.00291.

Van Slyke, D. M. (2007) 'Agents or stewards: Using theory to understand the government-nonprofit social service contracting relationship', *Journal of Public Administration Research and Theory: J-PART*, 17(2), pp. 157–187.

van de Ven, W. P. M. M. and van Vliet, R. C. J. A. (1992) 'How can we prevent cream skimming in a competitive health insurance market?', in P. Zweifel and H. E. Frech (eds) *Health Economics Worldwide*. Dordrecht: Springer Netherlands (Developments in Health Economics and Public Policy), pp. 23–46. https://doi.org/10.1007/978-94-011-2392-1_2.

Warner, M. E. (2013) 'Private finance for public goods: social impact bonds', *Journal of Economic Policy Reform*, 16(4), pp. 303–319. https://doi.org/10.1080/17487870.2013.835727.

Weber, M., Gerth, H. and Mills, C. W. (1948) *From Max Weber: Essays in Sociology*. London: Routledge & Kegan Paul.

Weber, W. L. (2014) *Production, Growth, and the Environment: An Economic Approach*. CRC Press.

Weiss, J. A. (1995) 'Review of reinventing government: How the entrepreneurial spirit is transforming the public sector; From red tape to results: Creating a government that works better and costs less', *The Academy of Management Review*, 20(1), pp. 229–235. https://doi.org/10.2307/258896.

Williams, J. W. (2020) 'Surveying the SIB economy: Social impact bonds, "local" challenges, and shifting markets in urban social problems', *Journal of Urban Affairs*, 42(6), pp. 907–919. https://doi.org/10.1080/07352166.2018.1511796.

Williamson, O. E. (1985) *The Economic Institutions of Capitalism: Firms, Markets, Relational Contracting*. New York: Free Press.

Wolf, C. (1979) 'A Theory of Nonmarket Failure: Framework for Implementation Analysis', *The Journal of Law & Economics*, 22(1), pp. 107–139.

Yukins, C. R. and Nicholas, C. (2023) The UNCITRAL Model Law on Public Procurement: Potential Next Steps. Edward Elgar. https://doi.org/10.2139/ssrn.4293959.

Acknowledgements

The authors are very grateful to the editors of the Elements in Public Policy Series, especially Judith Clifton, as well as to the two anonymous reviewers for their incisive feedback and recommendations; your collective input has greatly improved the piece. Further acknowledgement is owed to several generous colleagues – Alec Fraser, Anne Davies, Britt Regal, Carolyn Heinrich, Eleanor Carter, Ewan Ferlie, Mara Airoldi, Thomas Elston, and Mildred Warner – conversations with whom have illuminated and clarified many of the concepts discussed in this Element. Special dedication goes to our partners, Gregory and Hazel, and pets, Puffin and Marshmallow, for love and support throughout. This Element has been published open access with the support of King's Business School.

Dr FitzGerald led the development, drafting, and editing of this Element. Dr Macdonald contributed expertise on the legal foundations and practices in public procurement and their broader relevance to public administration. Any errors or misinterpretations are our own.

Public Policy

M. Ramesh
National University of Singapore (NUS)

M. Ramesh is UNESCO Chair on Social Policy Design at the Lee Kuan Yew School of Public Policy, NUS. His research focuses on governance and social policy in East and Southeast Asia, in addition to public policy institutions and processes. He has published extensively in reputed international journals. He is co-editor of *Policy and Society* and *Policy Design and Practice*.

Michael Howlett
Simon Fraser University, British Columbia

Michael Howlett is Burnaby Mountain Professor and Canada Research Chair (Tier1) in the Department of Political Science, Simon Fraser University. He specialises in public policy analysis, and resource and environmental policy. He is currently editor-in-chief of *Policy Sciences* and co-editor of the *Journal of Comparative Policy Analysis, Policy and Society* and *Policy Design and Practice*.

Xun WU
Hong Kong University of Science and Technology (Guangzhou)

Xun WU is currently a Professor at the Innovation, Policy and Entrepreneurship Thrust at the Society Hub of Hong Kong University of Science and Technology (Guangzhou). He is a policy scientist with a strong interest in the linkage between policy analysis and public management. Trained in engineering, economics, public administration, and policy analysis, his research seeks to make contribution to the design of effective public policies in dealing emerging policy challenges across Asian countries.

Judith Clifton
University of Cantabria

Judith Clifton is Professor of Economics at the University of Cantabria, Spain, and Editor-in-Chief of *Journal of Economic Policy Reform*. Her research interests include the determinants and consequences of public policy across a wide range of public services, from infrastructure to health, particularly in Europe and Latin America, as well as public banks, especially, the European Investment Bank. Most recently, she is principal investigator on the Horizon Europe Project GREENPATHS (www.greenpaths.info) on the just green transition.

Eduardo Araral
National University of Singapore (NUS)

Eduardo Araral specializes in the study of the causes and consequences of institutions for collective action and the governance of the commons. He is widely published in various journals and books and has presented in more than ninety conferences. Ed was a 2021–22 Fellow at the Center for Advanced Study of Behavioral Sciences, Stanford University. He has received more than US$6.6 million in external research grants as the lead or co-PI for public agencies and corporations. He currently serves as a Special Issue Editor (collective action, commons, institutions, governance) for World Development and is a member of the editorial boards of *Water Economics and Policy, World Development Sustainability, Water Alternatives* and the *International Journal of the Commons*.

About the Series

Elements in Public Policy is a concise and authoritative collection of assessments of the state of the art and future research directions in public policy research, as well as substantive new research on key topics. Edited by leading scholars in the field, the series is an ideal medium for reflecting on and advancing the understanding of critical issues in the public sphere. Collectively, the series provides a forum for broad and diverse coverage of all major topics in the field while integrating different disciplinary and methodological approaches.

Public Policy

Elements in the Series

Herding Scientists: A Story of Failed Reform at the CDC
Andrew B. Whitford

Public Policy and Universities: The Interplay of Knowledge and Power
Andrew Gunn and Michael Mintrom

Digital Technology, Politics, and Policy-Making
Fabrizio Gilardi

Policy Feedback: How Policies Shape Politics
Daniel Béland, Andrea Louise Campbell and R. Kent Weaver

Government Transparency: State of the Art and New Perspectives
Gregory Porumbescu, Albert Meijer and Stephan Grimmelikhuijsen

Relationality: The Inner Life of Public Policy
Raul P. Lejano and Wing Shan Kan

Understanding Accountability in Democratic Governance
Yannis Papadopoulos

Public Inquiries and Policy Design
Alastair Stark and Sophie Yates

Multiple Streams and Policy Ambiguity
Rob A. DeLeo, Reimut Zohlnhöfer and Nikolaos Zahariadis

Designing Behavioural Insights for Policy: Processes, Capacities & Institutions
Ishani Mukherjee and Assel Mussagulova

Robust Governance in Turbulent Times
Christopher Ansell, Eva Sørensen, Jacob Torfing and Jarle Trondal

Public Contracting for Social Outcomes
Clare J FitzGerald and J Ruairi Macdonald

A full series listing is available at: www.cambridge.org/EPPO

Milton Keynes UK
Ingram Content Group UK Ltd.
UKHW020007041224
452078UK00007B/515